In The Footsteps Of Jesus

Essays On The Contemporary Christian Journey

Volume 1

Richard Gribble, CSC

CSS Publishing Company, Inc

Lima, Ohio

IN THE FOOTSTEPS OF JESUS

FIRST EDITION Vol. 1
Copyright © 2019
by CSS Publishing Co., Inc.

Library of Congress Cataloging-in-Publication Data
Names: Gribble, Richard, author. Title: In the footsteps of Jesus : essays on the contemporary Christian journey / Richard Gribble, CSC.Description: First edition. | Lima, Ohio : CSS Publishing Company, Inc, [2019]- Contents: volume 1. God never gives up on us -- Chosen by God --
God is the "hound of heaven" -- Baptism: the call to discipleship -- Transformed to Christ -- Allowing God to change us -- God welcomes all -- Being open to God's call -- Jesus relieves us from paralysis -- Jesus: the gate to eternal life -- A fresh start in Christ -- Preparing the way of the Lord -- Seeking the light -- Moving from darkness to light -- Taking a chance on Jesus -- Keep your eyes on the goal -- Finding the lost -- Seeking God before all else -- Answering God's call -- Finding Jesus in all things -- Trust, the central virtue -- Trust as a manifestation of faith -- Persistence rewarded -- Perseverance wins the day -- Strength through weakness -- Bearing the cross with Jesus -- Reliance upon God -- God challenges us -- Nothing is too difficult for God -- Fear is useless, what is needed is trust. Identifiers: LCCN 2019011896| ISBN 9780788029486 (pbk. : alk. paper) | ISBN 0788029487 (pbk. : alk. paper) | ISBN 9780788029493 (ebk.) | ISBN 0788029495 (ebk.) Subjects: LCSH: Christian life. | Spiritual life--Christianity. Classification: LCC BV4501.3 .G7438 2019 | DDC 248.4--dc23 LC record available at https://lccn.loc.gov/2019011896

For more information about CSS Publishing Company resources, visit our website at www.csspub.com, email us at csr@csspub.com, or call (800) 241-4056.

e-book:
ISBN-13: 978-0-7880-2949-3
ISBN-10: 0-7880-2949-5

ISBN-13: 978-0-7880-2948-6
ISBN-10: 0-7880-2948-7

DIGITALLY PRINTED

Dedication

Walking in the footsteps of Jesus Christ has never been an easy task. Although the gospel evangelists tell us that Jesus' initial call to his chosen twelve apostles was met by an immediate response, the reality of being a disciple of the Lord was, in the end, certainly not lost on any of those initially chosen. Tradition tells us that all of them, save St. John, died as martyrs. Few if any of us will be called to give up our lives for our belief in Jesus, but walking in his footsteps, being his disciple, continues to be a significant challenge today. Thus, we need role models, present to us, who demonstrate by their words and actions that they not only desire to be Jesus' disciples, but are willing to walk the road less traveled and more difficult path that being his follower necessitates. I have been privileged in my life to meet a few people who are willing to "pay the price" that discipleship necessitates, but none as strongly and fervently as Christina Marie. It is thus appropriate that this book on discipleship be dedicated to her, for she indeed is one who daily walks in the footsteps of Jesus

Contents

Foreword

The popular and well-known poem *Footprints* describes a life lived in the footsteps of Jesus. The anonymous author of this timeless verse speaks of how, on a daily basis, the Christian walks alongside Jesus. Confident of the Lord's presence in his life, the man, when reviewing his life by observing their footprints in the sand, notes that "at the very lowest and saddest times in his life" only one set of footprints was observable. Bothered by the apparent lack of Jesus' presence at these critical junctures of life, he voices his complaint to the Lord. But Jesus responds, "My son, my precious child, I love you and I would never leave you. During your times of trial and suffering, when you see only one set of footprints, it was then that I carried you." This poem teaches an important lesson concerning the Christian life, namely that if we ask for the Lord's presence in our life, he will never abandon us, but rather will draw even closer, carrying us when necessary through and over the various storms and obstacles of life.

Walking the road of discipleship with Jesus, which is basic and generic for all Christians, has never been an easy task. On the contrary, all of the first Christians were ridiculed, harassed, and persecuted by both Jews and Gentiles alike. Saul of Tarsus was indeed intent on using every fiber of his being to obliterate followers of the "New Way," until Jesus appeared to him on the road to Damascus (Acts, Chapter 9). By his conversion, Saul, the great persecutor of Christians, became Paul the great apostle to the Gentiles. Even when the great Roman persecutions ceased after the Edict of Milan (313), the Christian road was never easy. The world's great allurements of power, wealth, and prestige, which have been manifested in various ways over the Christian era, constantly stand as temptations for the Christian to choose the world over God. Jesus' ability to overcome the world, successfully rejecting the great tempter Satan and his worldly enticements of success and materialism (Matthew 4:1-11), is illustrative of what we must do. Yet, even though he showed a perfect example, Christ realized the life of discipleship would not be easy. In fact, he claimed just the opposite: "If any want to become my followers, let them deny themselves and take up their cross and follow me. For those who want to save their life will lose it, and those who lose their life for my sake will find it." (Matthew 16:24-25)

The great privilege of being a disciple of Jesus incurs significant responsibility. We are blessed to have the word of God, the sacraments, the community of faith, and more. Yet, these great privileges incur significant responsibility. We have the responsibility to pray, to do our best to follow God's law as articulated by the church, and to be present to and celebrate with the community of faith on a regular basis. The Christian life of discipleship requires us to always walk in the footsteps of Jesus. This challenging road is accomplished by following a basic process. This book of essays, the first of two volumes, follows this basic process in its six part approach to walking in the footsteps of Jesus. In Part I, we learn that the Christian call is initiated by Christ. As God called Abram (Genesis 12:1-4), so Jesus called his apostles (Matthew 4:18-32). We, contemporary disciples of the Lord, began our Christian life through baptism, the initial action of God calling us. In Part II, we come to understand that the privilege of Jesus' call necessitates that we respond and seek the Lord in our life. Simply finding Jesus is, however, insufficient for if we are to be true disciples, we must place, as Part III suggests, our total trust and confidence in him. Once we find the Lord and entrust our lives to him, then in Part IV (within Volume 2) we learn of the Christian obligation to walk with him as best we are able on our daily journey of life. This journey of service and presence requires us, as seen in Part V, to fulfill the message that Jesus proclaimed and in Part VI to manifest the great qualities which he exhibited during his public ministry.

Our contemporary twenty-first-century first world environment does indeed pose significant challenges to walk in the footsteps of Jesus. We have so many places to go and so many things to do. Our availability is now 24/7; the busyness of life can be almost overwhelming. Thus, the tendency for many is to take a shortcut, the easy route, to accomplish whatever it is that we must do, or to achieve the goals we set. Yet, in his Sermon on the Mount, Jesus warned us that the easy way was a trap; the only viable way to be a true disciple was the more difficult path. He proclaimed, "Enter through the narrow gate; for the gate is wide and the road is easy that leads to destruction, and there are many who take it. For the gate is narrow and the road is hard that leads to life, and there are few who find it" (Matthew 7:13-14).

The challenges of contemporary society must prompt Christians to redouble their efforts to walk the daily journey of life in the footsteps of Jesus. We do this individually, but also as a community of faith, helping each other to find and remain on the one and only narrow path that leads to life eternal. Reflection upon and study of the scriptures can be an excellent vehicle to use on a daily basis to meet the challenges we face. This book can be utilized, individually, but especially in groups, to reflect upon the challenges of our day and ask ourselves how we can respond. We can certainly discover much by taking the time to reflect on God's word and pray for greater insight into its applicability in our daily lives.

It is my hope, therefore, that these essays will help you through prayer, our daily conversation with God, to believe that Jesus constantly seeks you, never leaving a stone unturned in a diligent search to bring you and all his children home to an eternal life with God. Once you understand the privilege of the Christian life and possess the conviction of God's eternal search for you, then our response can commence. First, however, we must trust and be confident that our walk with Jesus is the only road to salvation. Then we are challenged to fulfill his message and manifest qualities he demonstrated to a world so desperately in need of his presence. The privilege we possess is certain; our responsibility is equally sure. Let us respond with an open and generous heart; may our discipleship transform our lives forever.

Richard Gribble, CSC

Section I
Jesus Seeks Us

Introduction

Walking in the footsteps of Jesus Christ is indeed a great privilege, but with every privilege in life comes significant responsibilities. The life of discipleship with Jesus that we, the Christian community, desires is a process that begins with the realization that Jesus first calls us to walk with him. Thus, this most important journey of life, our daily task of walking in the presence of the Lord as his disciples, requires us from the beginning to listen for the call of the Lord. Scripture gives us numerous examples of this reality. This initial first step was made clear to the prophet Samuel by his mentor, Eli. The author of 1 Samuel (3:1) tells us "The word of the Lord was rare in those days, visions were not widespread." Thus, indeed it was a very special occurrence when God began to call the young lad Samuel to be a prophet. Initially, Eli did not understand, but when the Lord called the youth a third time he told him, "Go, lie down; and if he calls you, you shall say, 'Speak, Lord, for your servant is listening.'" (1 Samuel 3:9) In speaking with his apostles Jesus made it very clear who initiates the call: "You did not choose me but I chose you. And I appointed you to go and bear fruit, fruit that will last, so that the Father will give you whatever you ask in my name"(John 15:16). Jesus was the one who initiated the call to his inner circle, choosing Peter and his brother Andrew, James and his brother John (Mark 1:16-20).

As God called the prophets of the Hebrew Bible and Jesus called his apostles, so too does the Lord call you and me. There are few things in life upon which we can count absolutely, but the call of the Lord is certainly one. Jesus will call and he will leave no stone unturned in a diligent search for us. We think we can hide, but the reality is that the call of the Lord is omnipresent. During his public ministry, Jesus reached out and called not only those to whom he was initially sent, but later to outsiders when those first called rejected the invitation. No one was excluded from the call of the Lord. The powerful and influential, such as the Pharisees and Scribes, heard the message but their response was poor. Thus, as the parable of the great banquet (Luke 14:15-24) suggests, Jesus reached out to lepers, tax collectors, like Matthew, sinners, such as women caught in adultery and even foreigners, like Legion. Jesus' call was thus universal; he was willing to leave 99 perfectly well sheep to fend for themselves so as to find the one that had not responded to the call (Matthew 18:10-14).

The call of the Lord, experienced by some of the notables of history and literature, as manifested in the following reflections, is our privilege as well. God has a plan for each of his sons and daughters that cannot be frustrated. The call went to a double murderer, a forgotten Native American, a talented but drug-addicted writer and in the end each made their mark in history. The Lord's call comes to each one of us. The question, of course, for us is "Are we listening?" As our journey to walk in the footsteps of Jesus begins, let us, therefore listen as did Samuel for the call the Lord in our lives and respond "Speak, Lord, your servant is listening."

God Never Gives Up On Us

Theme: Challenges, hurdles, and obstacles of all sorts, whether it be ill health, financial difficulty, a wayward child or a loss of faith, are an endemic part of life. While it might be easy to "throw in the towel," give up and surrender, the Christian must always continue on the path, knowing that Jesus is with us every step of the way. He never gives up on us and one day will lead us to life eternal.

Scripture To Ponder: Exodus 32:1-15; I Corinthians 10:1--12; Luke 15:1-10

The name Robert Stroud is not commonly known in ordinary conversation, yet this man and his contribution to humanity will live on in the minds of many under a different title, the Birdman of Alcatraz. By nature, Stroud was not a congenial man. As a young person he was always getting into trouble: fights, disagreements and various altercations. When he was nineteen he was involved in a bar room brawl that led to the death of one man. Stroud was convicted of second-degree murder. Because the crime occurred on federal property, he was sent to the federal penitentiary at Leavenworth, Kansas to serve his sentence.

One might think that being in such a horrible environment as a federal prison would lead Robert Stroud to reform, to get his life in order. He continued, however, his former ways, being even more disruptive and troublesome. One day in the prison, a fight broke out among the inmates. Several guards got into the fray to restore order. In the process, Robert Stroud stabbed one of the guards using a little wooden knife which he had crafted in his cell. The guard died from the attack. The warden at Leavenworth thought the attack so onerous that he recommended that Stroud be executed for his offense; the jury at his trial agreed. Robert Stroud was scheduled to be executed in the electric chair.

Although it seemed Robert Stroud's fate was sealed, God had a plan for this man. The plan necessitated that he be alive and thus an intercessor arose in the form of Stroud's mother. Like any loving parent, Mrs. Stroud did not want to see her son die, especially such an ignoble death as execution in the electric chair. The only person who could commute Stroud's sentence was the President of the United States. Thus, Mrs. Stroud journeyed to Washington, DC to see President Woodrow Wilson. She was not able to see the president, but she did talk with the first lady. Mrs. Wilson in turn spoke to her husband on Stroud's behalf. Woodrow Wilson commuted Stroud's sentence to life in prison in solitary confinement. Robert Stroud was thus sentenced to spend the rest of this life without seeing any human beings, except the guard once per week when he was allowed the privilege of a shower. Even his meals were slipped through a special opening in his cell door.

But God had a plan for Robert Stroud; God never gave up on him. The manifestation of God's initial call began quite innocently one day when a small bird came and perched on the windowsill which looked out onto the Kansas countryside, Stroud's only contact with the outside world. Over time the bird came back. One bird turned into many birds. Stroud received permission to house these birds in his small cell. He read voraciously all the material he could obtain on birds and their care, especially diseases to which these animals were subject. Stroud conducted numerous experiments over several years. His study, research, and findings were collected into a book published in 1939 as *Stroud's Digest on the Diseases of Birds*. At the time it was the most comprehensive and authoritative study ever done on bird diseases and their cures.

Robert Stroud was a troublemaker; he was twice convicted of murder. Yet, God never gave up on him. God called and had a plan, a mission, for Robert Stroud. In the end, the plan was revealed and the mission was successfully completed.

Scripture speaks over and over about how God rejoices over one who returns to him, for God never gives up on anyone he calls, but rather continually seeks to bring his children home. God called the Hebrew people, never giving up on them; they always had another chance. The history of the Hebrew people is one of falling into and out of favor with God. This history had its beginning in the Exodus. God heard the cries of the people in bondage. Moses was raised up from among the people to be the deliverer. The Israelites were overjoyed at their rescue by the hand of God. But the joy and happiness of their deliverance was followed by betrayal.

A good example of this betrayal is found in the book of Exodus (32:7-14). The Israelites were frustrated by Moses' delay on Mount Sinai. Thus, they made and began to worship a golden calf. Angered by this act of idolatry and betrayal, God considers destroying the people of Israel and raising up for Moses another great nation. But Moses intercedes for the people and calms God's wrath. God relents in the punishment that was planned; the Hebrews will be given another chance.

Saint Paul was a man who was also given a second chance. We must remember that before his conversion, Paul, then named Saul, was a greater persecutor of Christians. In the Acts of the Apostles we read that Saul was present when Stephen, the first martyr, was being stoned. Luke, the author of Acts, tells us that Saul concurred in the murder of Stephen. In the first of the so-called "Pastoral Epistles," 1 Timothy 1:13a, Paul calls himself a sinner. We read, "I was formerly a blasphemer, a persecutor, and a man of violence." Yet, God dealt mercifully with Paul, as an extreme case, to give an example to those who would come later to the faith. Those later arrivals into the fold of faith are you and me, those who bear the name Christian and daily listen for God's call and seek to respond in appropriate ways. Paul is saying, through the example of his own life, that we should always believe that God is with us, caring for us. God wants us to be with him in heaven.

The gospels contain numerous stories and parables which describe how God never gives up on his greatest creation, human beings. One good example that illustrates this point is Luke 15:1-10. We see in this pericope two small vignettes, two stories about how happy God is when the lost are found. God goes in search for the one sheep in a hundred who may have strayed away. God searches for us like the woman searched for the one silver piece that had been lost. And when the sheep, the coin, or we are found, there is great rejoicing in heaven. That which belongs to God has been found; God's creation, made and called to be with God forever, has returned home.

At times we seem lost, but God is constantly there to guide us and to rejoice when we are found and return home. The life of faith we lead is a journey that is revealed daily. Sometimes it is easy to follow the Lord - the door appears fully open and the road seems clear. Other times, however, the door seems barely ajar and the road is filled with obstacles to impede our progress. Yet, if we trust in the Lord as did Mrs. Stroud, as did Moses and Saint Paul, then the way we need to proceed will be shown to us and the means to follow the path will be provided. God will give us the time and the talent we need to do his will and there will be great rejoicing in heaven when we find the way.

Our task is to open ourselves sufficiently to find God and, once God is found, to allow God to guide us. God rejoices when we are open. God will always call and give us, as he did with Robert Stroud, the Israelites and Saint Paul, a second, a third, a hundredth chance.

If God is there for us, we in turn must be open to God. Do we allow God into our lives? Does God have a chance with us? Do we believe, as Francis Thompson wrote in his famous poem *The Hound of Heaven*, that God pursues us without rest? More importantly, do we truly believe that God rejoices over our return to God's house?

There is a famous painting in the British Gallery in London with which many people are familiar. In the scene Jesus is in a garden. The Lord stands in front of a small cottage; he is knocking on the front door. There is nothing unusual about the scene except one important detail; there is no handle on the door. Jesus is knocking, one comes to understand, on the door of our hearts, a door that can only be opened from the inside. The book of Revelation tells us Jesus' thoughts at this moment, "Listen! I am standing at the door, knocking; if you hear my voice and open the door, I will come in to you and eat with you, and you with me" (3:20). God is knocking; are we prepared to answer? Let us today allow the God who never gives up on us to enter our hearts and permeate our lives. The dinner we will have will be the banquet of eternal life.

Questions To Ponder:

1. God is searching for me, but do I at times try to hide from God? Why?

2. How much pain and suffering am I willing to endure to continue on the road that leads to Jesus and life eternal?

3. What more must I do in order to give others the benefit of the doubt, a second chance. Why am I at times too judgmental in my association with those I encounter on the road of life?

4. What do I lack in faith that will allow me to believe and trust that God will lead me along the proper path?

5. What do I need to do in order to allow them into my life? Why am I at times a "do it myself" individual?

"I am the Lord, I have called you in righteousness, I have taken you by the hand and kept you" (Isaiah 42:6a).

Prayer: Lord, grant me insight to see you in our world and to accept your loving embrace.

Chosen By God

Theme: Human nature prompts us to follow certain instincts, including the desire to be recognized. When we do things well, achieve some goal, or complete some task, it is proper that we be recognized for what we have done. More importantly, however, is the realization that God has chosen each one of us to share his life and to pass that gift onto others. God recognizes us; we must do likewise for our brothers and sisters.

Scripture To Ponder: Isaiah 60:1-6; Ephesians 3:2-6; Matthew 2:1-12

In 1950, Jim Thorpe, a true "all-American," was selected by sports writers as the greatest athlete of the first half of the twentieth century. He was a star in the National Football League, perfecting the dropkick as an effective scoring weapon, and played professional baseball for seven years. He was a star in basketball, track and field, swimming, and lacrosse. Jim Thorpe may have been the greatest all-around athlete who ever lived, but this recognition in sport did not come without assistance and some pain.

Born in 1886 in the Indian Territory, now the state of Oklahoma, Thorpe lived with his family in relative obscurity. No one cared about him, his family, or his people, for to be a Native American in late nineteenth-century America was to be a nobody. Stereotyped as lazy and unproductive, Native Americans, like Jim Thorpe, were seldom recognized for anything that was positive. Through some good fortune, however, Jim was chosen to attend Carlisle Industrial School in Pennsylvania, a special college for American Indians. At Carlisle, Jim Thorpe would receive the recognition his athleticism deserved.

In the early years of this century Carlisle was a recognized school in major college athletics. Jim Thorpe's athletic ability was noticed by Glenn "Pop" Warner, Carlisle's legendary football coach. Jim had never seen a football, let alone played the game, but he was a natural. Carlisle played the Eastern football powerhouses of the day — Army, Penn, and Princeton — and with Jim Thorpe as their field leader the team triumphed over all, and, in the process, amassed one of the best records in the country. Thorpe was recognized as an all-American in 1911 and 1912.

Jim Thorpe excelled on the gridiron, but it was his extraordinary exploits in the 1912 Summer Olympics in Stockholm, Sweden, for which he will be best remembered. He entered and won the pentathlon (five events) and decathlon (ten events), the only athlete in Olympic track and field history to accomplish such a feat. The King of Sweden, when awarding Thorpe his gold medals, told him, "Sir, you are truly the world's greatest athlete." Jim Thorpe was a great athlete, maybe the best that ever lived. Yet, he needed to be called, to be chosen, in order to prove himself and his ability.

The call of the Lord to be disciples of Jesus is experienced in varied ways, but first we must know and feel that we have been chosen to be followers. Salvation history was initiated when God chose the Hebrew people to be uniquely his own. Isaiah speaks of God's plan of salvation, the roots of which are found in the special call of the Jewish people. In the third section of the book of Isaiah (chapter 56-66) we hear a vision for the Hebrews who have returned from exile in Babylon. "Arise, shine; for your light has come, and the glory of the Lord has risen upon you. For darkness shall cover the earth, and thick clouds the people; but the Lord will arise upon you, and his glory will appear over you. Nations shall come to your light, and kings to the brightness of your dawn" (Isaiah 60:1-3). From among the Jews who have been recognized by God as special among all peoples, one will arise, who will be recognized as great and special by those outside the kingdom of Israel.

Matthew's gospel (2:1-12) tells of the fulfillment of Isaiah's prophecy. Jesus, we recall, was recognized as someone special, not by his own people, but by outsiders. Astrologers from the

East came to Bethlehem and recognized Jesus as: 1) a king, represented by the gift of gold, 2) God, represented by the gift of frankincense, and 3) the one who will die so as to bring life to his people, represented by myrrh.

God's plan of universal salvation and recognition did not end with Jesus. Christ certainly provided the fulfillment of the Old Testament prophecy, but he passed on the gift of universal salvation to all. Saint Paul wrote to the Ephesians (3:5-6), "In former generations this mystery was not made known to humankind, as it has now been revealed to his holy apostles and prophets by the Spirit: that is, the Gentiles have become fellow heirs, members of the same body, and sharers in the promise in Christ through the gospel." Saint Paul told us that through Jesus we have all became co-heirs with the Jews. Christians bring God's loving plan of salvation full circle. God first recognized the special nature of the Jewish people. People from the outside recognize Jesus as special, a king, and at the same time divine. Finally, Jesus, the incarnate Son of God, who is king, extended the promise of universal recognition to all people. All people are special; all are called to answer the call to discipleship and through such a vocation inherit eternal life. Recognition is something we all seek; it is good to be noticed. If we do something well, whether it be in school, at our place of work, or in the civic community, we appreciate it when our efforts are recognized.

Recognition begins with self and then can move outward to others. Jim Thorpe believed in his own ability, but there was a need to combine this self-confidence with the call from others outside his immediate community. Thorpe was eventually universally recognized for his athletic achievement, but more importantly for us we must recognize that we have been chosen, called by God, and recognized as special in our role as disciples of the Lord. We have been called individually by name through baptism to lives of holiness and service. God has recognized our merit; we in turn must return the compliment and recognize others for who they are and what they do.

It is difficult at times in our contemporary society to recognize the beauty and distinctiveness of others; it is not the popular thing to do. Various aspects of diversity, such as the use of foreign languages, the presence of people of various ethnic origins, or the promotion of different philosophies of life, make recognition difficult for many. Sometimes people speak different languages, come from other nations, or have a different philosophy of life, which makes the recognition even more difficult. Sometimes we fail to recognize others simply because they think differently than we do. We are challenged to be more universal in our recognition and call of others. We are asked to be more Christ-like and recognize and appreciate others whom God has given us to share our lives. If we can change our attitudes and learn to accept others, then Scripture may be fulfilled for all, "Come, you that are blessed by my father, inherit the kingdom prepared for you from the foundation of the world" (Matthew 25:34b). God has chosen us and called us to be disciples of his son, Jesus Christ. Let us recognize the special nature of our call, be thankful for this great gift, and prepare ourselves to respond!

Questions To Ponder:

1. How do I answer the call the Lord in my life?

2. What have I done to promote and advance the dignity and cause of others I find on the road of life?

3. What more must I do to reach out to those who stand on the margins of society, those who others have rejected?

4. Before I love God and neighbor, I must love myself. What holds me back from appreciating my self-esteem?

5. When was the last time I recognized the accomplishments of others in a public way?

"I have called you by name, you are mine" (Isaiah 43:1b).

Prayer: Lord, grant me the strength to accept your call and the courage to carry it out.

God Is The "Hound Of Heaven"

Theme: "Those who persevere find victory," could easily be a model for life. Too often, however, we give up, we do not sufficiently engage or put in the effort that is necessary to complete tasks or foster relationships. Fortunately, God never gives up on us, but rather constantly, without rest, seeks our souls to bring them home. We must, in response, seek God as earnestly as he seeks us.

Scripture To Ponder: Acts 9:1-19; 1 Peter 3:15-18; John 14:15-21

"I fled him, down the nights and down the days; I fled him, down the arches of the years; I fled him, down the labyrinthine ways of my mind; and in the midst of tears I hid from him." So begins the famous poem *The Hound of Heaven* by Francis Thompson. The hound of Thompson's poem pursues us without a break; he is ever relentless in his search. The hound, which, of course is symbolic of God, pursues us in the heights of joy, the peak times in our life. God pursues us as well in the depths of sorrow, the great valleys of our life. We are pursued by God through the great successes of life and the failures as well.

The hound of heaven never gives up. Sometimes we try to hide from the hound. Sometimes we think we can escape his clutches. Sometimes we may even think that the hound has forgotten us and has given up. But the hound of heaven, our God, is ever present. God knows us; he is constantly calling and will never abandon us.

Francis Thompson himself experienced the dogged pursuit of the hound of heaven. Thompson was a drug addict on the streets of London in the early years of the twentieth century. Yet, he was a man who possessed great talent as a poet. Who would ever discover the skill he possessed and could share with the world? It was only through the pursuit of God that he was able to have his ability discovered by the proper people, leading him to clean up his life and make his significant contribution to the world of literature. Francis Thompson wrote from his own experience. God, the hound of heaven, pursued him without rest; he is doing the same thing for us!

As the poem and life of Francis Thompson demonstrates, so scripture speaks to us of how God calls and never abandons us. Jesus provided powerful images of how much God is willing to do, how far the Lord is willing to go in a diligent and never ending quest for our souls. Both Matthew (18:12-14) and Luke (15:3-7) told the popular parable of the lost sheep. Sometimes it seems that God does not make sense. After all in school 99% is awarded with a grade of A+; nary a person would not be overjoyed to have such a high return or success rate on any endeavor. Yet, 99% is not good enough for God. God leaves the 99 sheep that have no need for his service at the time and goes in search for the one who has strayed. God is the hound of heaven who leaves no stone unturned in a diligent and constant search for all of us, but especially those who have most need of God's attention and care. Following the lost sheep, Luke continues this same theme with a similar story of a woman who stops everything to search the house for one lost coin. Jesus summarizes the message of these two parables: "Just so, I tell you, there will be more joy in heaven over one sinner who repents than over 99 righteous persons who need no repentance."

Besides pursuing us, God provides for all our needs. God provides food - spiritual and real. The synoptics (Matthew 14:13-21, Mark 6:30-44, Luke 9:10-17) and John 6:1-15) tell the story of Jesus feeding the crowd of 5000 with bread and fish. The crowds were hungry and Jesus provided for their physical needs, but he provided more. In his famous "bread of life discourse" (John 6: 22-59), Jesus tells the people that he would feed them spiritually as well. Those who eat his flesh and drink his blood will gain life eternal. God also provides words, especially when we need them most. Jesus has promised us that when we are called upon to testify in his name, we will not be alone: "So make up your minds not to prepare your defense in advance; for I will give you words and a wisdom that none of your opponents will be able to withstand or contradict" (Luke 21: 14-15). God promised to send the paraclete: "This is the Spirit of truth, whom the world cannot receive, because it neither sees nor knows him" (John 14: 17a). Finally when Jesus ascended to heaven he promised "I am with you always, to the end of the age" (Matthew 28:20b).

We might ask an appropriate question as we observe the world around us. If God so diligently seeks after us, why is the world in the horrible state we see? Why is there a "war on terrorism?" Why is the situation in the Middle East seemingly unresolvable? Why are there so many problems in our churches? Has God been unfaithful? The answer is obvious. God is ever faithful, but what about all us? God allows the dynamism of our world, whether that is the dynamic forces of the created earth or the precious gift of human free will to operate as they were created. Thus, the reason the world suffers, the reason that the world is at times so difficult is because we have not been faithful.

As God pursues us so we must pursue God. We need to turn to God as the source of our strength. But in order to do this we must first allow God to come to us. God does not place us in handcuffs and order our obedience; the Lord does not place us in straitjackets and demand compliance. God does not come where he is not invited. Thus, we must first bid welcome to God. Then we can begin to pursue God as God pursues us. We must pursue God in prayer each day and stop making excuses for our failures. We must respond to God in our daily tasks with the understanding that a life of service is required of all the baptized. We must actively seek God as God seeks us!

The Spirit of God gives us life; the Spirit will never abandon us. As God pursues us and never relents in his search, so too must we pursue others, especially those whom God has given to us in special roles of responsibility. It is, for most, relatively easy to pursue those we like, those who do something for us, those who make us laugh and feel joyful. But how hard it can be to pursue those we find problematic or troublesome. But God is not exclusive in his pursuit of us; the hound of heaven searches for all without reservation. We must pursue members of our family, not only those we like, but maybe most especially those with whom we are estranged or find difficult. We must pursue our neighbor, whether that person lives down the street in our neighborhood or the individual who occupies the office next to ours at our place of work. We especially must pursue those whom society has cast off and placed on the margins - the aged, the infirmed, the stranger, alien or immigrant, the handicapped - all those who for whatever reason have been placed on the margins and have little if any chance to find the center and, thereby, the benefits of our contemporary society. God never gave a screening test to anyone, but rather relentlessly pursues our souls. We must do the same, if we truly are the hands, the feet, the active presence of God in our world.

Yes, the hound of heaven doggedly pursues our souls and never gives up. We must pursue God and one another. But in order to do this we must first be totally confident of God's call. Throughout salvation history God has been calling his people. He called the Jews and then from that community he called forth judges, kings, and prophets to lead the people. God continues to call us today. Let us today respond to the call of the Lord; let us open the door to our hearts and allow Jesus to enter.

Questions To Ponder:

1. How tenaciously do I pursue others as God pursues me?

2. What am I doing to further my relationship with the Lord? What more do I need to do?

3. What have I done recently to seek reconciliation with a person with whom I have a difficult relationship?

4. What can I do more directly to manifest my faith and fidelity to God in response to God's faithfulness to me?

5. What more do I need to do to meet the needs of my brothers and sisters who are less fortunate than myself?

"This brother of yours was dead and has come to life; he was lost and has been found" (Luke 15:32b).

Prayer: Lord, our God, never allow me to give up on anyone, including myself.

Baptism: The Call To Discipleship

Theme: Discipleship, walking the road of Jesus, must be a daily activity. We began this process of discipleship through baptism, but it is manifested in many ways, including our efforts at evangelization, our willingness to be reconciled to others, and the suffering we might endure in the name of Christ. Discipleship is the work of all Christians. Let us respond to this challenge.

Scripture To Ponder: Jeremiah 1:4-10; Acts 9:1-19; Luke 5:1-11

"And Jesus came and said to them, 'All authority in heaven and on earth has been given to me. Go, therefore, and make disciples of all nations, baptizing them in the name of the Father and of the Son and of the Holy Spirit, and teaching them to obey everything that I have commanded you. And remember, I am with you always, to the end of the age" (Matthew 28:18-20). The words of Jesus echo with a command, a privilege, and a challenge. The Lord challenged us to go forward as disciples and share his message with others. As God's children through baptism we are privileged to share God's life, but this privilege does not come without the consequent command to go forward. Baptism, the sacrament which unites all Christians in one family, the sacrament that initiates our call from the Lord, also unites us in the common call to discipleship.

The concept of baptism as a rite is rather straightforward, but the responsibilities that come with this sacrament are more complex. We all know that baptism makes us children of God and all the privileges that come with this elect position. Most people are not equally knowledgeable, however, about what baptism requires, or possibly we refuse to accept the responsibilities that come with the privilege. Baptism is a call to discipleship - but what exactly is discipleship?

Discipleship may be defined in many ways, but three principal aspects are crucial. To be a disciple first means to be a follower. Through baptism we become followers of Jesus and members of the church. Baptism next calls us to ministry, the work of a disciple. Lastly, discipleship requires that we become evangelists in response to Jesus' command to go and make disciples of all nations.

The process of being a follower of Jesus necessitates our total dedication to his principles and message. We cannot be a follower some days and one who goes it alone on others. Our mind must be fixed on the Lord. Saint Peter put it well," and baptism, which this prefigured, now saves you - not as a removal of dirt from the body, but as an appeal to God for a good conscience, through the resurrection of Jesus Christ" (1 Peter 3:21). Baptism is more than an act, it is a promise. Whether we knew it or not, our baptism bound us to Christ and the church. Thus, our attitude must be such as to seek union, with God and God's people.

Following Jesus is not easy; nobody said it would be. Dietrich Bonhoeffer, the famous Lutheran theologian who was executed by the Nazis at the end of World War II, knew that the price to be a true follower would be high. In his famous book, *The Cost of Discipleship* Bonhoeffer says that to be a disciple of Jesus will cost us everything in this life, but lead to eternal life. Bonhoeffer knew and believed what the scriptures say concerning our baptism into Christ's death and how it leads to life. Saint Paul wrote, "When you were buried with him in baptism, you were also raised with him through faith in the power of God, who raised him from the dead" (Colossians 2:12).

Hearing the call of the Lord and being his disciples requires us to minister to God's people. The tendency for many is to think that only certain people are called to ministry - one must have a vocation for such work. All the baptized, however, are called to work in the vineyard of the Lord. As scripture states, "The harvest is plentiful but the laborers are few; therefore ask the Lord of the harvest to send out laborers into his harvest." (Luke 10:2). We are the workers; we are the body of Christ. We are members of the priesthood of believers. Whatever our vocation, the single life, marriage and family, or religious life, we are all one through baptism. Again Saint Paul has written,"For in the spirit we are all baptized into one body - Jews, Greeks, slaves or free." (1 Corinthians 12:13a). As members of the one body, as brothers and sisters in the Lord, our ministry is a service to God and God's people.

Within the body of Christ we minister in specialized ways. Marriage places emphasis on ministry to spouse and children. Professionals can transform their daily work into ministry by an attitude of service to others. Single people also demonstrate ministry in their association with people around them. Those who are ordained possess a special invitation to discipleship.

Their vehicle to minister in varied ways, if done well, can touch many people. Ministers, through their presence and preaching, minister to all God's people and provide a special face to the presence of God in our world. This is the essential work of discipleship.

Evangelization is the third important aspect of discipleship. Jesus commands us to be evangelists, to go forth and spread his message. When we think of evangelization the image of the street-corner preacher comes to mind. Sermons of hellfire and brimstone and selling the faith door-to-door are other popular images. Evangelization is practiced in these ways, but there are less overt and more common ways in which we bring others closer to God, which is the essential ministry of the evangelist.

Evangelization is practiced in the active life of the minister. As has already been mentioned, ministry and service are not optional works for the Christian; all are called to work in God's vineyard. How many of us have been touched by the works and service of others? When we see someone who reaches out to another, like the late Mother Teresa or Desmond Tutu, we are challenged to go the extra mile for those who need our assistance. The actions of others force us to act; their service becomes an instance of evangelization. Active ministry and service to others is something in which we can participate each day. There are formal ministries in the church and the community, but more commonly, service is performed in everyday events which few think is significant. Courtesy in our manner of life, calmness in a time of strife, using conciliation over argumentation in time of conflict are all ways of demonstrating service to others and ministry in God's kingdom on earth.

Another important method of evangelization is the process of reconciliation. The ability to admit one's brokenness, especially before another, is an act of evangelization. How many times have we been inspired and had our hearts lifted by seeing another turn away from evil and begin a new path which leads to God? Baptism is a rebirth into the life of repentance. Scripture states that John the Baptist came as a precursor of the Lord to provide a baptism of repentance for the forgiveness of sins (Mark 1:4; Luke 3:3; Acts 13:24). When one turns away from sin and begins anew, the value of such an act is incalculable. Repentance and reconciliation require courage and provide a challenge for others to seek a similar road in their lives.

Reconciliation is a means of evangelization and discipleship. The courage to honestly face one's human brokenness, imperfection, and sinfulness is of immeasurable witness value to others. Like the reaction of the forgiving father in parable of the prodigal son (Luke 15:11-32), we are moved in emotion and brought closer to God by the humility of a fellow human. Receiving God's forgiveness and our reconciliation with God's people, the body of Christ, empowers us through a renewed spirit to bring God's message of love to all. Thus, reconciliation becomes a vehicle for evangelization.

Baptism as a call to discipleship is an active sacrament; it is anything but passive. This first sacrament calls us to be followers, ministers and evangelists; it calls us to listen for the Lord. We must live the vocation of holiness to which we have all been called. Our call is to be members with all the privileges that come with being part of God's family. Our membership gives us responsibilities as well. We must go forth actively to do God's work in our world. Baptism is the original call from God to a life which seeks to bring others closer to God. May the baptism which we all share, our common denominator in the faith, allow us to be disciples and show the face of God to others.

Questions To Ponder:

1. What must I do to more completely fulfill my responsibilities as a baptized Christian?

2. How do I manifest my life of discipleship on a daily basis?

3. With whom must I seek reconciliation as a form of discipleship? What must I do to be reconciled with this person?

4. What have I done recently to bring the word of God to others? Am I active or too passive in my daily living of the faith?

5. How far am I willing to go to profess my faith and discipleship in Christ?

"When they [James and John] had brought their boats to shore, they left everything and followed him" (Luke 5:11).

Prayer: Lord, help me to be your disciple in all that I say and do.

Transformed To Christ

Theme: On the human level we are always seeking to be transformed. We want to be transformed in our physical appearance, our mental acuity, our social consciousness, and our personal discipline. The one true transformation, however, that we all must seek is to be transformed into a greater, deeper and more faith-filled relationship with Jesus Christ, for it is this relationship that will one day bring us home to life eternal.

Scripture To Ponder: Judges 6:34-40; James 4:11-12; John 3:1-21

Many years ago, on a beautiful Sunday afternoon, I was walking with a friend in San Francisco's fabled Golden Gate Park. As we were conversing, a young man approached and in a polite but energetic tone of voice asked, "Are you saved?" Both of us were taken aback, especially my friend who was a semi-practicing Jew. His question prompted me to respond, "I certainly hope so." But he pressed on, "How do you know; when were you saved?" The point of the man's query was for me to identify specifically the time I was converted, transformed or said, "yes" to Christ as my personal Savior. The question can be posed more generically: Are you seeking transformation in your life; are you open and ready for a renewed relationship with Jesus? Are you listening for the call of the Lord?

The need for transformation is a major theme of holy scripture and is presented as an on-going process of individual, spiritual, and personal change. The concept of being "born again" lies at the very heart of the New Testament. The call of Nicodemus by Jesus in John's gospel is the classic example. Nicodemus comes to Jesus at night; he stands in the darkness. Jesus says, "Very truly, I tell you, no one can see the kingdom of God without being born from above" (John 3:3). Nicodemus does not understand, thinking initially that Jesus is referring to a physical re-birth, but

Jesus corrects this misconception to speak of being re-born in the Spirit. The point of the text is that Nicodemus needs a spiritual rebirth, a personal transformation.

Dying and rising lies at the heart of being born again, that is our personal transformation. In his book, *The Heart of Christianity: Rediscovering a Life of Faith*, theologian Marcus Borg says that personal transformation requires a new heart. Personal transformation in one's life can serve as the bridge between what he terms the "earlier" and "emerging" paradigms of religious understanding, those who are more traditional in their personal piety and religious practice, and those religiously-formed in a more contemporary church, which is highly influenced by science, historical scholarship, religious pluralism and cultural diversity. Dying to old self and rising to a new identity, one that is transformed to the mission and message of Christ, is the substance of this new heart. This theme is pervasive in the New Testament. Mark's gospel (8:34b-35) sets the tone: "If any want to become my followers, let them deny themselves and take up their cross and follow me. For those who want to save their life will lose it, and those who lose their life for my sake and for the sake of the gospel, will save it." This equates discipleship with taking up the cross. For the synoptics, (Matthew 16:24-25, Luke 9:23-24) the path of personal transformation is the path of death and resurrection.

The path of personal transformation through death and resurrection is carried beyond the synoptics. In Saint John's gospel besides the story of Nicodemus, Jesus also described the path of personal transformation: "I tell you, unless a grain of wheat falls in the earth and dies, it remains just a single grain; but if it dies, it bears much fruit." We can never maximize our potential as Christians if we hold back and save ourselves. It is the very act of giving ourselves away that allows us to bear fruit. Saint Paul's letters also have numerous references to dying and rising as a metaphor for personal transformation. For Paul the goal is to be "in Christ"; the way to achieve this is dying to our old self and being reborn in Christ. He wrote, "More than that, I regard

35

everything as loss because of the surpassing value of knowing Christ Jesus my Lord. For his sake I have suffered the loss of all things, and I regard them as rubbish, in order that I may gain Christ, and be found in him, not having a righteousness of my own that comes from the law, but one that comes through faith in Christ, the righteousness of God based on faith" (Philippians 3:8-9).

Personal transformation is easy to affect on the outside, but of little value. Many remember the popular Broadway stage play, *Damn Yankees*. The protagonist, Joe Hardy, was a middle-aged "couch potato," who regularly watched his beloved Washington Senators play and generally lose to the dreaded New York Yankees. Wanting badly to play ball, Joe, in a moment of frustration, sold his soul to Satan for the privilege to play for the Senators. Joe did well and so too the Senators, but he missed his old existence; he wanted out of his pact with Satan. Joe was transformed, but only externally; he was not converted in his heart.

We need transformation, not on the outside like Joe Hardy, but rather, a true and permanent conversion on the inside, a conversion of mind and heart. This must have been what happened to Peter, James, and John on Mount Tabor when they observed Jesus in his transfigured state. All the synoptics (Matthew 17:1-8, Mark 9:2-8, Luke 9:28-36) reported that Jesus was momentarily transformed into a radiance beyond human description. Yet, Jesus returned to his normal appearance. What, however, happened to Peter, James, and John? They were transformed on the inside. From that moment forward they would never be able to see Jesus as a man only; he was God. Their minds and hearts were transformed. This is the transformation we must seek.

What does being transformed to Christ mean in a practical way? First, it means experiencing the call of the Lord. Next, we must change our attitudes, making them more Christlike. We should care less about ourselves and more about the common good. Too often we make decisions and judgments based almost exclusively on personal welfare and benefit, but one of the basic teachings in Catholic social thought is to promote the common good over individual need. We must acquire patterns of thought that are based on equality and openness. While members of the human community are different in many ways, we are not better or worse, just different. Far too often people equate difference with superiority or inferiority. Since we are all made in the image and likeness of God, we are equals. As Saint Paul put it, "As many of you as were baptized into Christ have clothed yourselves with Christ. There is no longer Jew or Greek, there is no longer slave or free, there is no longer male or female; for all of you are one in Christ Jesus" (Galatians 3:27-28).

Once our way of thinking has been transformed to Christ, then we must change our actions. In essence we must be converted to the need to be active participants in God's plan. A passive response is no longer viable. The Epistle of James provides one of the best examples of the need to be transformed to an active living of God's word. People who only listen and do not act only deceive themselves; they are not fooling God. James provided an image (1:23-25) of how we deceive ourselves by self-observation in a mirror. When we look into the mirror we see all the imperfections, blemishes, and problems. If the individual forgets what is seen in the mirror, the situation cannot be corrected; things will remain in disarray.

James told us that we must live the word of God; we must be transformed to an active relationship with Christ. The apostle continued by saying that we cannot be true practitioners of the faith we profess if we cannot bridle our tongue. James would say, *think before you speak*. A wise elementary school teacher put it this way to his class, "Engage mind before putting mouth in gear." Furthermore, we are not simply to talk about what we will do, but to care for orphans and widows in their distress. Again, James must have remembered or been told about Jesus words, "Truly I tell you, just as you did it for one of the least of these who are members of my family, you did it for me" (Matthew 25:40b). Any other approach is self-deception making our religion worthless.

The question, "Are you saved?" woke me up one Sunday afternoon to a deeper realization of my need to be transformed. All Christians must take the sometimes perilous inward journey to see what needs to be changed in attitude and action so that we can be transformed and conform our lives more closely to Christ. Let us listen for the call of the Lord, take the journey, have the courage to change, and through our efforts draw ourselves one step closer to God's promise of eternal life.

Questions To Ponder:

1. What must I do to be more conformed to Christ?

2. What do I need to do so as to be better able to hear the voice of God in my life?

3. What interior transformation is necessary in my life so as to be truly transformed?

4. What must I do to assist in the transformation of others, so they can find the message of Christ in their lives?

5. How does God speak to me through the voice of others?

"Very truly, I tell you, no one can see the kingdom of God without being born from above" (John 3:3).

Prayer: Lord, allow me to be open to your gentle and loving touch, transforming my heart to make it more like your own.

Allowing God To Change Us

Theme: Self-determination is a strong drive for all of us. The free will that God gave us prompts us to seek control of our lives at all time. However, at times we have no control; at other times God wants to challenge us to change, but we do not listen. Allowing God to transform us is an absolute necessity for the Christian life.

Scripture To Ponder: Genesis 12: 1-4; 2 Timothy 1:8-10; Matthew 17:1-9

"Hoke, you are my best friend." It took Daisy Werthan almost twenty years to make that statement; it wasn't easy. The relationship between Daisy and Hoke was not mutual or cordial at the outset. Daisy had driven her beautiful 1948 Packard through a fence and into her neighbor's backyard. Boolie Werthan, Daisy's son, thought that such an incident was sufficient evidence to warrant that his mother stop driving, but she was still active and thus needed a driver, a chauffeur. Hoke Coleburn, a middle-aged African-American man, was Boolie's choice for the job. Daisy, however, would not accept this restriction, this change in her life; she was not open to the call of the Lord to be transformed.

Boolie may have hired Hoke but that did not mean that Miss Daisy had to use his service. As Hoke stood idly by, Miss Daisy took the street car wherever she went, to the hair dresser, to the grocery store. Hoke Coleburn was being paid for doing nothing and that is precisely how Miss Daisy wanted things.

As stubborn as she could be, Miss Daisy ultimately did change her attitude. One day she needed a few things from the store. She left the house and began to walk toward the street car. Hoke decided that Miss Daisy's refusal to use his services needed to end. As she walked down the sidewalk Hoke slowly drove alongside in the new 1948 Hudson, Boolie had purchased for his mother. "Where are you going?" scowled Daisy. Hoke replied, "I'm fixin' to take you to the store!" Although still not content with the arrangement, Daisy agreed to get into the car; her conversion had begun.

Daisy did not approve, but Hoke had become her chauffeur. Whether it was to the temple, you see Miss Daisy was Jewish, the store, or a trip to Mobile, Alabama, to visit relatives, Daisy and Hoke went together. As the years passed their relationship as driver and passenger grew; they became bonded together. Then one day Miss Daisy's long and sometimes difficult conversion became complete with her statement of faith, "Hoke, you are my best friend."

Alfred Uhry's 1988 Pulitzer Prize winning play and popular movie *Driving Miss Daisy* is more than a story of a chauffeur and an elderly rich widow. It speaks of the process of transformation and acceptance in one's life. Scripture challenges us to listen for the call and to transform our lives in order to gain greater personal knowledge and understanding of God.

The book of Genesis (12:1-4) describes how Abram was asked by God to go forth, to venture out, to find change, and be converted. What God asked of Abram could not have been easy. He was an old man, yet he was asked to leave his home, his livelihood, everything that he knew. God had given him a promise, a special blessing, that he would be the father of a great nation one day. Even with such a promise, however, Abram would not have been able to act if he had not been a man of faith. Abram was able to believe that God was calling him to change for some good reason.

In a similar way, Naaman, who was a leper from Aram, was transformed by God. He initially took offense at the request of the prophet Elisha to simply wash seven times in the Jordan in order to be cured. However, he eventually was convinced by his servants to obey the prophet and was cured. So amazed was he at this turn of events that he stated that from henceforth sacrifice should only be offered to the God of Israel. (2 Kings 5:11-18)

The Christian life is a constant challenge to welcome the opportunities for transformation that enter our lives. We can look at three traditional disciplines of our faith and see how they can help us along the path which leads to transformation in our lives. Almsgiving is the first discipline. We need to believe that works of mercy are necessary. How can we change our schedules or daily lives so as to make almsgiving something that is possible in what we do? Do we need to change our attitudes about almsgiving which may hold us back from full participation?

Fasting is a second discipline. Do we need to change our eating habits permanently? Do we need to eliminate certain items from our life, things which ultimately cause us harm - drugs, drink, tobacco? Can we transform our lives to be in solidarity with those who are less fortunate than most of us when it comes to material possessions?

Prayer is a third traditional Christian discipline. Can we change our priorities if needed so as to assure we make time for conversation with our God, today and each day? Are we willing to try new methods of prayer in order to make our conversation with the Lord more fruitful and fulfilling? Can we let the word of God become part of us, to enter deep down into us so as to later blossom forth as God's love directed toward others?

Each day we have the opportunity to encounter the Lord. As we journey along the Christian road, let us allow the encounters we have with God change us; let each encounter be the opportunity for transformation. Let us accept the change that God asks of us, like Abram, like Naaman, like Miss Daisy in Alfred Uhry's play. Let our encounter with God change us forever!

Questions To Ponder:

1. What aspect of my life needs to be transformed the most?

2. In what ways can I discipline myself so as to transform my life to one more consistent with the message of Christ?

3. Why do I avoid the challenges that God sends my way, opportunities to transform my life?

4. What opportunities have I missed because of my refusal to listen to the call of God in my life?

5. What more can I do in order to prepare myself for the future challenges that will come my way?

"Rend your hearts and not your clothing. Return to the Lord, your God" (Joel 2:13).

Prayer: Father, help me to be open to the conversion which only you can bring.

God Welcomes All

Theme: Receiving the appreciation and welcome of others is something we all appreciate. If we have been away from home or have done something well, it is natural that we seek some type of recognition. Too often, however, we do not afford the same welcome or appreciation to many members of our society, especially those who are new, different, or unattractive. God, however, calls us to welcome all, but especially the most vulnerable in our society.

Scripture To Ponder: Isaiah 56:1-7; Romans 11:13-15,29-32; Matthew 15:21-28

The "War to end all wars," the great World War I, created a problem of displaced persons that the world had never seen. In 1917, refugees and orphans abounded. Everywhere one turned, the streets of cities and towns were filled with people who "did not belong." Because the war was fought in Europe, this human dilemma was greatest there, but that did not mean that things were fine here in the United States. For reasons that are very complicated this period of American history saw an alarming rise in the numbers of homeless children. Most were cast-offs from homes. For reasons many times unknown children were released by parents and loved ones. They were forced to fend for themselves, to live on the streets as best as they were able to do. Nobody seemed to care about these children.

There was however, one who cared. His name was Edward Flanagan, a priest from New York. Father Flanagan decided that something needed to be done for the children of this country who were cast-offs, who had been forced, for one reason or another, into a life on the streets. Flanagan purchased 1500 acres of land in eastern Nebraska near Omaha. He invited homeless boys, those rejected, those who had no one, to come to his new facility. No one was a foreigner or outsider to Edward Flanagan.

Starting in 1917 the little settlement began to grow. By 1936 the property had been incorporated into a village. By 1980 this village, known as Boys Town, a place for those who had nobody else, had over 600 residents.

The work of Father Edward Flanagan and his establishment of Boys Town illustrates the idea of how God accepts all, whoever we are, whatever we have done. Writing to the Hebrews after their return from exile in Babylon, Isaiah speaks of how God welcomes all people. Isaiah emphatically stated that the people must do what is just; they must hold to God's law. "All who keep the sabbath, and do not profane it, and hold fast my covenant - these I will bring to my mountain, and make them joyful in my house of prayer. (56:7a) Hebrews and foreigners are called by God. God's house is a house of prayer for all who choose to come. This certainly must have been a difficult teaching for the Hebrews to swallow - after all they were the chosen people. Now God says that all are welcome.

Matthew's gospel (15:21-28) demonstrates how the mission of God has expanded to all people. A Canaanite woman asked Jesus for a favor, a miracle. Canaanites were outsiders; they lived east of the Jordan River. As foreigners they were not welcome. Jesus said that his mission was to the lost sheep of the house of Israel. In other words, Jesus said his time was to be spent in bringing back the ten lost tribes of Israel; his mission was to the ancient Hebrews. The woman was persistent, however. Her perseverance and the cleverness of her response to Jesus' statement were rewarded. Jesus, through his action of curing the Canaanite woman's daughter, extended his mission, his ministry to all. Jesus accepts all; none are rejected. All people receive the call; all can receive the gifts of God.

Most certainly God welcomes us all. God created all and rejects nothing, no person, no thing. Parish communities of faith are good examples of how God accepts all. People come from different ethnic groups, are of different races, and have different states in life, and yet they gather together in prayer and work together in service. God accepts us for who we are today, not what we were yesterday, not what we will be tomorrow. God accepts us as we are, namely sinners struggling to further our relationship with God.

The only thing that can separate us from God is ourselves. In his letter to the Romans, Saint Paul powerfully spoke of God's abundant mercy to all people. He said that the gifts and mercy of God were irrevocable. God has given us free will and with that gift we sometimes don't fully live up to our Christian calling; we are sinners. Yet, as Paul said, God made us in disobedience, imperfect in other words, so that he could show mercy to us. God wants to be merciful. His arms are open on the cross; he waits for our return. If we have failed, it is because God created us as imperfect beings. There is nothing, absolutely nothing, that God cannot forgive, except that for which we fail to ask forgiveness. Saint Paul (Romans 8:38-39) said this so powerfully: "For I am convinced that neither death, nor life, nor angels, nor rulers, nor things present, nor things to come, nor powers, nor height, nor depth, nor anything else in all creation, will be able to separate us from the love of God in Christ Jesus our Lord."

Since God forgives and welcomes us, we must do the same to those who enter our lives. We must be forgiving to those who hurt us, whether that be physically or psychologically. People will ignore us; this must be forgiven also. People at times will make our lives very difficult and uncomfortable. Jesus asks us to love them in return. Our task in life is to be bountiful in mercy to others and ourselves as God is with us.

Let us today welcome the foreigner, the refugee, the outcast. Let us in turn allow God to call us. God the ever powerful and merciful one has gifts and forgiveness that can never be lost. Let us accept the loving embrace of God this day!

Questions To Ponder:

1. What efforts do I make to welcome others as Christ welcomes us?

2. When was the last time I went out of my way to meet the needs of a stranger, especially one who is poor and/or has been rejected by society?

3. What new possibilities or opportunities have I rejected simply because they originate from people I do not know?

4. With whom do I need to be reconciled? What can I do to build a bridge between myself and that person?

5. Why do I close my eyes and act as if I do not see the challenges that many in our society face?

"For whoever does the will of my Father in heaven is my brother and sister and mother" (Matthew 12:50).

Prayer: Lord, help me always to find you in my sisters and brothers.

Being Open To God's Call

Theme: Physical impairment of any kind may limit some activity, but the blindness, deafness, or refusal to meet the needs of our sisters and brothers are much more deadly forms of impairment. God has given us abilities to reach out and meet the needs of our brothers and sisters, especially those most in need. Let us meet the challenge that God's call to holiness may require of us.

Scripture To Ponder: Amos 6:4-7; James 5:13-20; Matthew 25:31-46

Today it is obvious when we encounter a person with a physical handicap. If we are walking down the street and we see a person approaching us using a red-tipped cane we know the individual is blind or at best severely visually impaired. If we are on the bus, the subway, or other forms of public transportation and we see two people communicating using sign language, we know those people are deaf and/or mute. When we see a person in a wheelchair we know that for whatever reason - birth defect, accident or other situation - the person cannot walk or their movement is severely impaired.

Such physical handicaps are readily observable in others, but there are many other handicaps we all face that are much less discernible or even hidden, yet may be more problematic and destructive than any physical inability.

Jesus cured many physical handicaps, opening the eyes of the blind, and the ears of the deaf, freeing the tongues of the mute and allowing the lame to walk, but he did much more. Saint Luke's (18:35-43) description of Jesus' cure of a blind man near Jericho is a good example. In response to the man's request, "Lord, let me see again," Jesus restores the man's sight, not only physically but spiritually for the evangelist tells us that the man followed Jesus and glorified God. When Jesus cured the man

47

who was mute (Matthew 9:32-34) those witnessing these events "were amazed and said, 'Never has anything like this been seen in Israel.'" Similarly when Jesus cured the paralytic, (Mark 2: 1-12) the people glorified God. In all these examples, Jesus' cure of some physical disability led to a deeper and more important spiritual transformation that probably was not realized.

Many of the Jews, especially the religious elite, were spiritually handicapped in their understanding and vision of Jesus. Their physical faculties worked fine, but their spiritual blindness, deafness, and lameness kept them in a darkness and silence that did not allow them to move forward. In many ways this "paralysis" was worse than any physical problem could create.

Like the Jewish religious elite, most people today have the great fortune of possessing all their faculties and senses. Surely, many people wear glasses or contact lenses to aid their visual acuity; some people need the assistance of a hearing aid. As we grow older it becomes physically more difficult to run as fast, compete as stridently or possess the endurance that we had as youths on the athletic field. But, for the most part, we possess all of our basic abilities, limited though they are at times by age and circumstance.

Still, we must admit that while our physical senses and movements may not be seriously impaired, we are, nonetheless, blind, deaf, mute, and lame to many of the needs of our world. We choose not to see, to hear, to speak or to move forward in our lives, but seem content in our present reality. Yet, the message of scripture is very clear: we must be neither complacent nor indifferent to the cries of the marginalized in our society who seek justice. We must be open to God's call in its many manifestations.

Our physical ability to see challenges us to look beyond our limited personal purview to the needs of the world around us. When we observe problems or situations that require our attention, we simply cannot close our eyes and hope that by some miracle the situation will disappear or rectify itself. Too often we go about as if we were blind; we refuse to see what is around us. We cannot stand idly by and claim ignorance of the reality around us when we see the face of poverty, observe discrimination, or acknowledge that injustice is real and pervasive. When we learn of great need, whether that means assisting after some natural disaster, financially aiding a group or individual, or hearing the cries of the poor, we cannot play deaf to the situation.

Complacency is unacceptable in a world which badly needs our assistance. The prophet Amos (6: 4-7) warned the religious leaders of his day against being complacent. "Alas for those who lie on beds of ivory, and lounge on their couches, and eat lambs from the flock, and calves from the stall; who sing idol songs to the sound of the harp, and like David improvise on instruments of music; who drink wine from bowls, and anoint themselves with the finest oils, but are not grieved over the ruin of Joseph! Therefore they will now be the first to go into exile, and the revelry of the loungers shall pass away." We may be complacent by our failure to see or our refusal to listen, but most prominently by our lack of initiative, the sins of inaction and omission.

Life provides us all sorts of opportunities to act in a positive way on behalf of another, to speak the words that must be spoken or simply to listen and be present to a person in need. Most especially, however, we are provided opportunities to do something for another. Possibly we can run an errand for someone, visit one who is sick or help a person who has too many tasks and insufficient time to complete them. Too often we act as if we are handicapped in some way. Jesus is very clear about the consequences for those who fail to assist their brothers and sisters in need. In the famous last judgment scene of Matthew's gospel, (25:44-46) the challenge is placed before us: "Lord, when was it that we saw you hungry or thirsty or a stranger or naked or sick or in prison, and did not take care of you? Then he [the king] will answer them, 'Truly I tell you, just as you did not do it to one of the least of these, you did not do it to me.' And these will go away into eternal punishment, but the righteous into eternal life." Failure to meet the needs of those around us, to feign a handicap, will lead to our personal destruction and loss of salvation.

The scriptures are very clear about our need to open all our senses to the reality that is around us, to listen to the call of the Lord in its various manifestations. While it may be relatively simple to discern a physical handicap of a person we encounter, it is much more difficult and certainly more important to recognize the hidden handicaps of our own lives. We should never trick ourselves into thinking that God is not well aware of our failures to act when we had the opportunity to lighten the load of one of God's anawim. May we be aware of our need to see, to hear and never to be complacent in meeting the needs of God's people. Our positive steps will make life today better for our sisters and brothers, will assist in building the kingdom of God in our world, and, in the end, will bring us the gift of eternal life, God's promise to all who believe.

Questions To Ponder:

1. What have I done recently to lighten the burden of a brother or sister in need?

2. Why am I blind and/or deaf to the cries of those around me? Why am I afraid to act?

3. Why am I so fearful to encounter and assist those who are less privileged than me, economically, educationally, socially, or physically?

4. Why am I complacent or reticent to act when an opportunity to assist one in need comes my way?

5. Why do I become psychologically "paralyzed" when a situation or someone challenges me to move beyond my "comfort zone?"

"So faith by itself, if it has no works, is dead" (James 2:17).

Prayer: Jesus, help me to never be complacent, especially when my neighbor asks for my assistance.

Jesus Releases Us From Paralysis

Theme: While our physical senses of sight, hearing, touch, and smell may work fine, we are at times unknowingly paralyzed in our spirituality or fear of things new and different. If we allow him to guide us, however, Jesus can and will release us from any and all of the paralyses that plague our life. Let us be open, therefore, to the possibilities that Christ can bring to us.

Scripture to Ponder: 1 Samuel 16:1-13; Ephesians 5:8-14; John 9:1-41

Anne Mansfield Sullivan truly was a miracle worker. Partially blind from birth, she managed to overcome this handicap and graduated from the prestigious Perkins School for the Blind in Boston. The miracle which was the life of Anne Sullivan, however, had very little to do with her own handicap; it had everything to do with the multiple handicaps of a young girl. Thus, the miracle began on March 2, 1887 when twenty-year-old Anne Mansfield Sullivan met six-year-old Helen Keller.

Helen was born in 1880, a healthy and strong child. At nineteen months of age, however, she contracted a disease which left her blind, deaf, and ultimately mute. Helen Keller lived in a world of total darkness and silence. Helen's parents, frustrated in their inability to aid their daughter, sought the counsel and advice of the famous inventor of the telephone, Alexander Graham Bell, a man who knew adversity from his own problem with hearing loss. Bell knew Anne Sullivan and arranged for the first meeting between student and teacher.

Anne Sullivan's task was monumental - how could she enter into the world of darkness and silence which was the reality of Helen Keller's existence? First, she had to gain Helen's confidence which was accomplished with relative ease. The next step, however, would be much more difficult. Anne Sullivan needed to teach Helen that her multiple handicaps, her inability to see, hear, and speak, were not impediments at all. Rather, her condition afforded her the opportunity to see, hear, and speak in new and different ways, to communicate on another level. Helen Keller could not see images; she could not read the words on the printed page. But she could feel and, thus, learned to read braille. Helen could not hear or speak, but she did learn to finger spell and sign in order to communicate with others.

Helen Keller learned her lessons well. In fact, she learned so well that in 1904 she graduated cum laude from prestigious Radcliffe College. She went on to be a successful author and an internationally known celebrity who aided the cause of handicapped people throughout the world. It was the life of Anne Mansfield Sullivan, however, which in many ways was the true miracle. She opened the mind of Helen Keller to a world of possibilities.

Anne Sullivan could not cure Helen's physical blindness, deafness, or inability to speak, but she was able to break through the silence and darkness by curing her emotional and possibly spiritual paralysis. While the majority of people are fortunate to possess all their senses and faculties, we are nevertheless, often unknowingly, many times paralyzed in more critical ways. Scripture challenges us to consider our paralysis and find ways to liberate ourselves.

The story of Jesus' encounter with the paralytic (Matthew 9:1-8; Mark 2:1-12; Luke 5:17-26) presents a good illustration of how the physically handicapped are in a better state than those who live in psychological or spiritual paralysis. In the story Jesus has attracted such a crowd that it is impossible for the friends of the paralytic to present their comrade to Jesus. They feel the call of Jesus and thus use their ingenuity to open the roof above the Lord and lower down their friend directly in front of him. The evangelists set up two contrasting attitudes in the story. The friends of the paralytic are open to the call. They can see, hear, and move, not only physically but more importantly psychologically and spiritually. They fully believe that Jesus can act on their friend's behalf. The Pharisees and teachers of the law, on the other hand, are paralyzed. It seems they can see, hear, and move quite well, but unlike the friends of the paralytic they are psychologically and spiritually blind, deaf, and lame. They are paralyzed in their attitudes and beliefs. They do not want to believe that Jesus can act, that he has the power to forgive sin.

Another powerful story that contrasts those who are physically and psychologically paralyzed is Saint John's account (11:1-44) of Jesus raising Lazarus from the dead. John tells his readers that Jesus, upon hearing of Lazarus illness, intentionally waited three days before making his way to Bethany. Jesus says there was a reason for this delay: "This illness does not lead to death; rather it is for God's glory, so that the Son of God may be glorified through it" (11:4b). Jesus realized that spiritual death was much worse than physical mortality and, thus, he allowed Lazarus to die. But he later says, "Unbind him and let him go." Jesus realized that many of those present were spiritually dead, tied to the past - to problems, circumstances, and other things of the world. Thus, in freeing Lazarus from physical death, Jesus encourages all those present to release themselves from the past and any circumstances that keep them from spiritual freedom.

It is clear from these two stories that Jesus considers psychological and spiritual paralysis more severe than physical problems. Thus, we must consider our own lives and see that although we may be able to see, hear and move - that is we have our faculties - yet we are paralyzed in spiritual ways that inhibit the growth we need in our relationship with God. Yes, some see and hear better than others. Day-by-day our physical abilities seem to become less; it is a law of nature. The physical limitations manifest themselves in varied ways and we must be concerned with these realities, but should we not be more concerned as Jesus suggests in the scripture with our spiritual and psychological paralyses that plague us in so many ways.

We are psychologically paralyzed in several ways. We are trapped in certain ways of doing things. We have a method that works for us and, thus, no other plans or ways of doing things will be considered. We are trapped in our attitudes and opinions -

about others, institutions, groups, or ideas. We know we are right and, thus, everyone else is wrong. There is no need to change. We are trapped in our knowledge. We possess a certain level of expertise in an area and are content to stay at this level. This is especially true with our faith knowledge. We use the knowledge we gained as children and say, "Why should I learn more?"

We are paralyzed spiritually as well. We are trapped in our prayer life. We know our prayer is not helping; we experience no growth. Yet, we won't change, try something new, seek guidance, or assistance. We have a certain level of comfortableness and we won't change for anyone or anything. We are tapped in our image of the church; we don't want to see other possibilities. We live in a black and white fantasy when the reality is that a significant level of gray exists. Yet, this seems to have no merit in our thinking.

We are all paralyzed in varied ways, but fortunately there is a way out; we have a solution. Isaiah the prophet (35:1-10) describes an idyllic setting where the blind can see, the deaf can hear, the mute can sing, and the lame run like stags. The idyllic environment that Isaiah describes cannot be achieved passively. On the contrary, we, like Anne Mansfield Sullivan, like the friends of the paralytic, must actively seek to cast out the darkness, silence and paralyses in our lives. We must remove the blinders and ear plugs that keep us in ignorance; we must listen for the call. Comfortable lives can lead to complacency, stagnation, and ultimately death. Let us, therefore, actively seek to find God. Jesus said, "Unbind him and let him go." Let us accept the release that God brings us this day!

Questions To Ponder:

1. How much time do I take to observe social problems and injustice in my immediate world, and the greater world community?

2. Why am I at times complacent in my attitude saying, "It is not my responsibility?"

3. What prompts me to tie myself to the past; why will I not allow myself to be free?
4. What can I do to release others from the various spiritual paralyses from which they may suffer?

5. Why do I fear the possibility of change in my life? What holds me back from trying new things?

"But be doers of the word, and not merely hearers who deceive themselves" (James 1:22).

Prayer: Lord, grant me the grace to recognize problems in our society and the strength to make the world a better place.

Jesus: The Gate To Eternal Life

Theme: Modern life in our first world society fills us with temptations of a temporal nature. Whether it is power, riches, or prestige, it is easy to be swayed and enamored by these contemporary "gods." We must be cautious, however, for these can easily lead us astray, driving us away from God and toward the world. We must always be focused, therefore, on the eternal values of God.

Scripture To Ponder: Jeremiah 17:5-8; 1 Corinthians 15:12-20; Luke 6:17-26

Three sisters, who were kind, generous, and possessed great faith, lived in a cabin in the hills. One day while working in the backyard garden the sisters unearthed a large box. When they removed the top they saw it was filled with gold coins. They all shrieked loudly, "Beware of the soul-taker!" They were uncertain what to do - should they cover the box up and pretend like nothing had happened or should they flee from the house?

It so happened that four young men had recently moved into the cabin next door. They heard the commotion at the sisters' home and went to investigate. The sisters informed their neighbors, "We are trying to flee from the soul-taker." "What's a soul-taker?" one of the men responded. "Please show us." The sisters took the men into the backyard and, pointing at the box of gold coins, said, "That is the soul-taker!" The men laughed under their breath and said to one another, "They think the money is a soul-taker." One of the men said to the women, "If you ladies are so frightened, please go to town for a few hours and we will take care of the problem for you." The women agreed and left immediately.

The men made their plans. First, they decided to split the money four ways. Then they determined that two men would stay and completely unearth the box of gold while the other two went to town, bought some food, and made plans for a quick escape. The two who stayed began to think, "It would be better to split the money two ways; we will receive more." Thus, they decided to ambush their friends when they returned and kill them. The two who went to town had similar thoughts. They decided to poison the food and feed it to their compatriots. Then they would bury their bodies in the hole where the box had been and split the money between them.

When the two men from town returned they were abused and killed by their friends. But before the bodies were buried, the two murderers decided to eat the food provided since it was fresh. They soon became sick and died. When the sisters returned they found the four men dead and the box of gold still there. "We told them it was a soul-taker, but they refused to believe." The women immediately made plans to leave their home.

What is the source of our sustenance? What provides direction for our lives? What do our actions and words tell others about the priorities in our lives? These questions and others are raised in this Armenian folktale of the sisters and their box of gold. Scripture provides many similar challenges.

Jesus was very explicit in the gospels in telling his followers the proper direction of our lives. While we all know there are many options, there is only one that leads to life; there is only one true call. In John's gospel (14:6), Jesus proclaimed, "I am the way, and the truth, and the life. No one comes to the Father except through me." Earlier John (10:7b, 9) quoted Jesus, "Very truly, I tell you, I am the gate for the sheep.... Whoever enters by me will be saved, and will come in and go out and find pasture." Jesus provides the proper direction to life through his life and teaching. There are many other paths, but these routes, while highly traveled and seemingly less problematic, only lead people astray. Jesus was aware of this problem. In the Sermon on the Mount (Matthew 7:13-14), Jesus warned the crowd, "Enter through the narrow gate; for the gate is wide and the road is easy that leads to destruction, and there are many who take it. For the gate is narrow and the road is hard that leads to life, and there are few who find it." Jesus did not promise us a rose garden; rather he warned us that suffering and pain would be our lot (Matthew 10:16-23). Yet, for those who listen for the call and persevere, the gift of eternal life awaits.

Contemporary life provides a seemingly endless list of possibilities. When we reach the proverbial "fork in the road", it generally has more than two options. The increasing complexity of society provides many different paths and, thus, often our process of making decisions is more challenging. Yet, when we boil down the many options of our lives, they come to two common denominators - the option for the world or the option for God. The choice is not always black and white; there is much gray that must be negotiated. Still, we have sufficient maturity, faith development, and knowledge to discern between the things of God and the world. Thus, a choice must be made. This is the existential option. God has given us free will, the ability to say yes or no at all times to any request or invitation. The Christian must ultimately choose God, the only path to life.

This special path, the way of God as opposed to the ways of the world, is for all people of faith. St. Peter came to realize this through the vision that he describes in the Acts of the Apostles 11:1-18. The Jews, as the chosen people, quite naturally thought they had an inside track with respect to salvation in the new way of Jesus. But as the apostle said, "God has given even to the Gentiles the repentance that leads to life" (11:18b). Like Peter, we must be open to the reality that God has called all to this special path. Christians have the obligation as well as the distinct privilege to lead others along this path, but we can only do so by physically witnessing, through the things we do and say, that we have made a total and permanent commitment to the one and only path to life.

The people of God hold a special responsibility to provide an example, a model of the path that must be followed. We know all too well our own foibles and sinfulness, but others are often not so understanding. Thus, we must always be conscious of the way people see us and how what we do and say affects them. We cannot demonstrate an attitude like the men in the story of the gold coins, seeking our sustenance from the things of the world, whether that be material possessions, opportunity, position, or worldly prestige. Yet, as humans we get caught up in what we do and who we are. Unconsciously at times we fall into the trap that our work or ministry, our position, or the responsibilities we hold become our sustenance as surely as the gold was thought to be the sustenance of the men. The sisters were right, if we are not careful these things, which at times hold such fascination to us, will become our soul-taker. These are false paths that take us away from the direction we must seek. We need to re-concentrate our efforts toward finding Jesus, listening for his call, and entering through him, the sheep gate. It seems so simple and we can easily say we are following the proper road, but have world responsibilities and opportunities become the gold, the false god of our lives?

Each day is an opportunity to re-center ourselves on the things, people, and ideas that are of true importance in our life. We must find and walk again the lesser traveled path, so as to enter through the narrow gate that leads to life. This is the more difficult path, but the best things in life are almost always the most challenging. Let us keep our priorities straight, stay clear of the contemporary soul-takers so we will be prepared for Jesus, whose presence we need and whose return we await.

Questions To Ponder:

1. Which of my daily actions are the things of the world and which are those of God?

2. How do I model the life of Christ and his message in my daily words and actions?

3. What is the principle source of my spiritual sustenance?

4. Why at times do I find such fascination with the temporalities of this world and ignore the eternal ideas and values of God?

5. What is the contemporary "soul-taker" that has greatest attraction for me?

"[Jesus said], in the world you face persecution. But take courage; I have conquered the world" (John 16:33).

Prayer: Lord, help me to always choose you over the world

Section II

Responding To Jesus' Call

Introduction

It is abundantly clear, as evidenced in scripture and manifested in the lives of millions who have walked in the footsteps of Jesus, that the call of the Lord is universal, but the next critical step, our response to Jesus is totally up to us. Christ places no one in a straitjacket, forcing us to respond. Rather, through the great gift of free will, the Lord allows us to freely accept or reject his call. As unbelievable as it sounds, God trusts us so much, loving us beyond all our capability to understand, that he will allow us to make the choice to walk in his footsteps or choose another path.

It is abundantly clear, again as seen in scripture, history, and literature, that numerous individuals have taken up the challenge of Christ, followed in his footsteps and by their actions made the world a better place. Reluctant prophets such as Moses, who was not a gifted speaker, Amos who proclaimed that he was a shepherd and a dresser of sycamores, Isaiah, who claimed that he was unqualified, and Jeremiah, who protested that he was a mere youth, nevertheless all responded to the call of God to go forth and proclaim his word. Their ministry of prophecy, leading the Israelites to the promised land and indicting the religious and civic elite of their day, telling them of God's displeasure with their leadership, was anything but easy, but somehow they drew confidence from the call and their own inner strength to respond generously. The apostles as well were in essence asked by Jesus to leave everything behind and to follow in his footsteps. They too, we are told, immediately left behind their former ways of life, took a leap of faith and became the first to walk beside Jesus.

Twenty-first-century society forces us to move at a rapid pace and to engage almost daily a highly competitive environment. This situation requires us to prioritize how we will utilize the limited time, energy, and opportunities we are given. We are pulled in numerous ways, by our jobs, family, civic responsibilities and, of course, God. Responding to the call of the Lord requires us to make a purposeful decision, choosing God as the highest priority of our life and placing other needs and opportunities, as important as they may seem, somewhere down our list of priorities. Our response to the Lord will require much of us, both in belief and action, but therein lays the great challenge.

Responding to the call of the Lord has been manifested in numerous ways. Sometimes tragedy strikes and we're asked to pick up the pieces and move forward. On other occasions, oppression, whether of individuals or of groups forces us to boldly proclaim our discipleship in Jesus, moving ourselves and others from the darkness to the light. At other times, we simply have to take a chance, believing that the call of the Lord is always present, and if we will have the courage to respond, the Lord will take care of us. We must always, as well, keep our eye on the goal, namely eternal life with Christ, an end which requires us to respond to the initial call. Responding to the call of the Lord will also require us to seek out those in our society who have been lost, shunned, or placed on the margins. Our response might be early or late, but what is essential is to respond. Saint Peter put it well, when challenged by Jesus whether he and the other apostles would leave him, proclaiming, "Lord, to whom can we go? You have the words of eternal life. We have come to believe and know that you are the holy one of God" (John 6:68). Let us, with equal confidence, respond with generous hearts and open minds to the call of the Lord.

A Fresh Start In Christ

Theme: Adversity and failure will, sooner or later come in our lives. Financial difficulties in business, serious or incapacitating illness for ourselves or others, even death of a loved one, or loss of one's job can obscure our intended Christian path. With faith in God, however, and with our own perseverance, we can overcome such challenges and, as necessary, begin anew. With Christ, nothing is impossible.

Scriptures To Ponder: Isaiah 61:1-7; Philippians 3:8-14; John 8:1-11

Thomas Alva Edison, the famous inventor of the electric light and so many other modern conveniences of our contemporary world, was a man who experienced the beauty of a fresh start, but it was not one that he expected. One day Edison's laboratory, located in Orange, New Jersey, caught fire. Inside were all of his experiments, notes, and various projects upon which he was working. Basically his whole professional life was in the building. Because the structure was built of bricks and concrete it was insured for only $200,000, since most believed it was fireproof. As the fire raged, Edison, a man in his early sixties, watched as his world was enveloped in fire and smoke. His longish white hair was tossed about by a gentle breeze.

Edison's son, observing his father, could not believe what was happening. His father was not a young man; it would be very difficult to start over again. The next day, after the fire had been extinguished, the elder Edison began to sift through what remained to see if there was anything that could be salvaged. However, it was a total loss. At the time he told his son, "It is a good thing that we had the fire; it burned up all my mistakes." In a rather amazing reality, one week to the day of the fire, Thomas Edison presented to the world the first phonograph, the predecessor of stereo, MP-3 players and similar devices with delight our ears with music. From the ashes of destruction, Edison found a fresh start.

The scriptures present numerous examples of individuals and groups who, after tragedy or some significant event, have re-started their lives and oriented them more toward God; they responded to the call of the Lord. The classic story in the Hebrew Bible of Job illustrates this idea best. We are told that Job was one of the richest of men, with flocks, herds, and crops that abounded, plus a wonderful family with many sons and daughters. But God allowed all of his "wealth" to be lost as a test. In the end, after enduring tragedy and suffering, Job's riches were restored in ways greater than he originally possessed.

A new beginning was experienced by the Hebrews during the period of the Babylonian Exile. Taken from their homeland and sent in exile to Babylon for fifty years, the community eventually returned and under the direction of Ezra and Nehemiah rebuilt not only the temple, which was emblematic of the restoration of their faith, but also their personal lives. Isaiah (65:19-20a, 21) expressed this restoration well: "I will rejoice in Jerusalem, and delight in my people; no more shall the sound of weeping be heard in it, or the cry of distress. No more shall there be in it an infant that lives but a few days, or an old person who does not live out a lifetime; … They shall build houses and inhabit them; they shall plant vineyards and eat their fruit."

The New Testament also provides ample examples of new beginnings. Jesus' encounter with the woman caught in the act of adultery (John 8:2-11) is one good example. Refusing to condemn the woman, Jesus told her to go forward, but from henceforth avoid such sins. The call of the apostles was certainly a fresh beginning. After receiving the invitation from Jesus, these unlearned fishermen (for the most part) immediately left their families and way of life and became dedicated disciples of the Lord. Jesus' charisma and message were so strong that they struck out in a completely new direction after their initial encounter with him.

Nicodemus, a member of the Jewish Sanhedrin who came to Jesus at night, was another person who found fresh beginnings by responding to Christ. While initially not understanding Jesus' message that one must be born again, that one must find a new direction in life, Nicodemus eventually got the message, for he was present after the crucifixion, performing the ritual anointing of Christ's body (John 19:39).

Along the journey of life, we will experience many events or encounter individuals or groups who will force us to seek new beginnings. Crises of health, whether they be personal, family or close friends, especially ending in death, force us to begin anew. Widows and widowers, parents who have lost children, and those who experienced the death of a loved one through accident or war, know the need to begin anew. The pain of separation or divorce requires major adjustments and a new start, for both parents and children. Loss of job or financial problems of any nature cause great crises in families. Living on less, adjusting lifestyle, moving to another location, or even the need to accept aid from outside sources again prompts reflection and the need to start again. It is difficult to pick up the pieces of our lives after we have been shattered. But Christians cannot allow evil, in all of its various manifestations, to defeat us. Rather, through trust in God and significant individual effort, along with, when necessary, the assistance of others, we must rebuild our lives.

Sometimes, like Job, we will be even more successful than before. Situation and circumstance often lead us into avenues of life that we would rather not travel. But the road of life is never a straight line between two points; rather we travel in a circuitous route, often retracing our steps, making wrong turns, and even taking a few detours. But through perseverance, hard work, and confidence that the Lord is with us every step of the way, in the end we can respond to Jesus' call and find new beginnings.

As Thomas Edison was able to start afresh from the ashes of his burned out laboratory, so too must we seek a new start when crises of any nature come our way. As Jesus calmed the storm at sea, (Mark 4:35-41) and in the process amazed the apostles, so will he right the ship of our lives when storms, problems, tragedy, and the various vicissitudes of life, throw us off course. The Lord will always do his part, but we must have trust and confidence that he will act. Edison's story and the many examples of Scripture must inspire us to respond to the Lord's call, to stay on the road. Let us do our part; Jesus will take care of the rest.

Questions To Ponder:

1. When adversity strikes, how have I responded to the call of the Lord who suffered many trials for me?

2. What do I need to do to discover new beginnings in my life, regardless of the situation in which I find myself?

3. As a Christian, what have I done to assist those who are starting over or seeking another path in life?

4. Have I accepted the changes and novelty that new people, especially immigrants, bring to my life and our society?

5. What must I do to blaze a new direction in my life? Am I directed toward Christ or to the world?

"The Lord gave and the Lord has taken away; blessed be the name of the Lord" (Job 1:21b).

Prayer: Lord, help me to respond with generosity when the road is rocky and the path unclear.

Preparing The Way Of The Lord

Theme: Whenever we travel, we prepare for the journey. The more extensive the trip, the greater is our preparation. The most significant journey for all Christians is our return to God, yet too often our preparations are inadequate. We must take the time and make the effort to properly and completely prepare for our return to God, the one from whom we came and the one to whom we are destined to return.

Scripture To Ponder: Baruch 5:1-9; Philippians 1:4-11; Luke 3:1-6

One day a mighty and majestic pine tree, the tallest tree in the whole forest, said to a little squirrel playing in its branches, "There is a great treasure waiting for you at my top most branch, if you are willing to make the journey in order to find it." Now this great pine tree was itself a great treasure. It produced some of the meatiest and tastiest pine nuts in the forest and it provided shelter for many animals that called the forest home. This little squirrel was inquisitive, however, and she wondered what the great treasure might be. She decided at that moment that she would take the journey so as to discover the great treasure.

The trip would be long and because the squirrel was wise and possessed forethought, she knew planning was required. Food had to be taken on the journey. Thus, she chose from her nest some of the "meatiest" nuts that she had stored. She placed them in a little satchel and tied it around her waist. Then she began to climb. At the base of the tree the branches were full and the pine nuts were plentiful, but as she rose higher and higher in the tree, the branches became thinner and thinner and the pine nuts fewer and fewer. She stopped for a moment and rested. She was happy that she had brought food along on the trip. She took out a nut and enjoyed a little snack. This trip was more difficult then she had anticipated. She thought about returning home, but the commitment had been made and she would complete the journey.

As she climbed higher and higher she wondered what the great treasure might be. Maybe she should have asked the tree. But when she looked up she thought she saw the top. There was no need to ask now; soon she would find out for herself. After another half hour of climbing she made it to the top and clung to the top most branch as it swayed in the wind. She looked around for the treasure, but could see nothing. She thought there might be a giant pine nut or at least one which was delightful to the eye; she saw nothing like this. Had the tree tricked her? Disappointed, frustrated, and now tired and hungry, she prepared to return home. Thus, she turned around, hung upside down, as squirrels often do, and made ready to climb down. But when she looked down the view that she beheld was truly amazing. She could see for miles, every valley and mountain, every stream and river. Because this was the tallest tree she could see without any obstruction. This was better than any pine nut could possibly be.

She wanted to stay there forever, but realized because the climb had been long and difficult that the sun would set in a few hours and she needed to return home by nightfall. Thus, renewed in spirit, if not in body, she made the easier trip down the tree. That night when speaking to all the other squirrels, she told them about her adventure, and it is said by all her friends that she was never hungry again.[1]

Like the squirrel who undertook a difficult journey in order to find a great treasure, so all the Christian community moves day-by-day along the path which leads to the discovery of the greatest treasure of all — Jesus Christ. We should know that peoples long before our time took similar journeys in order to find God. Scripture tells us about these journeys.

Baruch was a prophet who spoke to the Hebrew people in exile in Babylon. The people had been away from their homeland

---

1 Paraphrased from in John Aurelio *The Squirrel and the Pine Tree*, Colors! Stories of the Kingdom (New York: Crossroad, 1993), 63-64.

for a long time; many probably thought that God had abandoned them. Baruch tells the people that if they want to find God and return home they must build a highway. It is not a highway made of cement, asphalt, and stone, like the roads of today. No, this is a highway in their minds. The prophet writes, "Arise , O Jerusalem, stand upon the height; look toward the east, and see your children gathered from west to east at the word of the holy one, rejoicing that God has remembered them. ... For God has ordered that every high mountain and the everlasting hills be made low and the valleys filled up, to make level ground, so that Israel may walk safely in the glory of God. ... For God will lead Israel with joy, in the light of his glory, with the mercy and righteousness that come from God" (Baruch 5: 5-7,9). The reason the people could not find God was that their minds were too full of other things; God was not that important. Baruch tells the people to remove those things that are unimportant and make a path to God that is level, smooth, and straight. Then the people will find God and they will return home.

John the Baptist was another prophet who delivered a similar message to a different group of people. John spoke to the Hebrews of his day and told them that they too must build a highway in order to find God: "Prepare the way of the Lord; make his paths straight. Every valley shall be filled, and every mountain and hill shall be made low; and the crooked shall be made straight, and the rough ways made smooth" (Luke 3:4b-5). Jesus, the one for whom John was to prepare the way, was present, but the people would not find him unless they prepared themselves.

We have all learned in high school geometry that the shortest distance between any two points is a straight line. Life is full of journeys which require us to move between points A and B. Some of the journeys are physical and it may be possible to move in a direct path, a straight line. But the most important journeys in life, such as our journey through school, the road of moving from the single life to marriage and family, or our movement from being a working person to retirement, are seldom if ever negotiated in a straight line. No, we rise to the heights of success and triumph and we at times enter the valley of defeat and despair. We come to a fork in the road and we choose the right path only to find that it is really a detour and more difficult and time consuming than if we had chosen to go to the left.

We must do the best we can to make level, smooth, and straight our highway that leads to God. The little squirrel realized that her long journey would require some planning and thus she brought food along with her. The church provides opportunities to prepare ourselves as we journey toward God. We have the liturgical seasons, scripture, and the Christian community itself. These give insight, guidance, and strength on our journey to seek the Lord and find salvation and eternal life with God.

All of us, like the squirrel are on the tree and we are climbing toward our goal of seeking the Lord. God willing, we will make it to the top. But when we get there, turn upside down and look out what will we see? Hopefully we can see the enormity of God's love manifest in so many ways, all of which help to guide us home. Let us continue on the road blazed by Christ and the countless saints who have followed his path. Let us walk the road to Jesus and eternal life.

Questions To Ponder:

1. What is lacking in my faith that prevents me from taking the more difficult, yet only true path to God?

2. What obstacles do I need to remove from my life that hinder my journey to the Lord?

3. What is the status of the highway that I need to build between myself and God? Is it progressing, stalled, or does it lack the proper materials for its completion?

4. What is lacking as I prepare myself for my ultimate journey home to God?

5. What prompts me to take detours on my journey home to God, especially when I know the proper path?

"Enter through the narrow gate; for the gate is wide and the road is easy that leads to destruction, and there are many who take it. For the gate is narrow and the road is hard that leads to life, and there are few who find it" (Matthew 7:13-14).

Prayer: Lord, help me to walk the road less traveled, but the only path that leads to you.

Seeking The Light

Theme: Contemporary life can often seem very dark. Crime, corruption in business and government, personal or family financial or health issues, and at times loss of faith can paralyze us, preventing us from being the people God calls us to be. Fortunately, Jesus, the light is ever present, but we must have the faith to seek the light that will ultimately bring us back home.

Scripture To Ponder: Isaiah 61:1-11; 1 Thessalonians 5:16-24; John 1:6-28

South Africa, a nation rich in resources, people, and possibility only recently emerged from its darkest hour. The nation traveled through a tunnel of darkness and ignorance that was generated by a social and racial system of segregation called Apartheid. The National Party of South Africa, formed in 1914 after a revolt by the Afrikaner people against the British, created the system of Apartheid in 1948. Ostensibly it was advertised as a means for "separate development" but in essence it was a system designed to maintain white supremacy. Apartheid did not allow 77% of the nation's people, namely the black citizens, to participate in the government. South Africa's dark night lasted almost fifty years, but there was a ray of hope.

The first streaks of light were found in a courageous white politician, F.W. De Klerk. De Klerk had risen to the top of the National Party and was elected president of South Africa in 1990. He believed that the Apartheid system was unjust and inhumane and, thus, he immediately took steps to dismantle it. He needed help, however; he could not do it alone. He found his assistant in the person of Nelson Mandela, a black man whose name had been closely associated with freedom for many years.

Mandela, a member of the African National Congress, was convicted in 1964 of a capital crime and sentenced to life in prison. Despite his incarceration, he kept the flame of faith alive that one day there would be freedom in his native land. That day began in February 1990 when De Klerk ordered Mandela to be released.

The two men, different in many ways, began to work together to find a common way toward peace and justice. They negotiated a settlement between the National Party and the African National Congress that led to the composition of a new constitution and the transition of power to a more democratic form of government. In 1993, De Klerk and Mandela shared the prestigious Nobel Peace Prize. The next year, Nelson Mandela was elected the first black president of South Africa.

Like the United States, which suffered through its dark night of slavery and Civil War, so did South Africa experience the dark tunnel of Apartheid. It took the combined efforts of two men, Nelson Mandela and F.W. De Klerk, to keep the light of faith burning and thereby bring their nation to a new day.

Society today often seems shrouded in darkness and uncertainty; we wonder at times where the light has gone. Scripture clearly tells us that we must rejoice for the light of Christ is always near. We must open our eyes, ears, and hearts in order to recognize him and respond to his call. The book of the prophet Isaiah is divided into three sections, prophecy proclaimed before, during, and after the infamous Babylonian exile. The Hebrew people experienced a deep and dark night in their exile, their fifty years away from their homeland. The prophet (61:10) tells those who have returned from exile that it is a new day and it is time to rejoice: "I will greatly rejoice in the Lord, my whole being shall exult in my God; for he has clothed me with the garments of salvation, he has covered me with the robe of righteousness, as a bridegroom decks himself with a garland, and as a bride adorns herself with her jewels."

The Hebrew scriptures provide many other examples of our need to seek the light, which is God. The psalmist (Psalm 27:1) writes, "The Lord is my light and my salvation; whom shall I fear? The Lord is the stronghold of my life; of whom should I be afraid?" and again (119:105) "Your word is a lamp to my feet and a light to my path." The prophet Micah (7:8) speaks of his trust in God, the light: "Do not rejoice over me, O my enemy; when I fall I shall rise; when I sit in darkness, the Lord will be a light to me."

The light of faith, forecast by the prophets of ancient Israel, was inherited by the Christian community, as articulated in the New Testament, which also presents us with a clear message of our need for the light, a missive that is most clear and dramatic in the corpus of Saint John. In the famous prologue to his gospel (1:1-18), the apostle speaks of John the Baptist as the precursor who prepared the world for the light, Jesus, who "shines in the darkness and the darkness did not overcome it." (1:5) Jesus said of himself, "I am the light of the world. Whoever follows me will never walk in darkness, but will have the light of life" (8:12). Again, he proclaimed, "I have come as light into the world, so that everyone who believes in me should not remain in darkness" (12:46). John summarizes his message on the importance of seeking the light in his first letter (1:5-7): "This is the message we have heard from him and proclaim to you, that God is light and in him there is no darkness at all. If we say that we have fellowship with him while we are walking in darkness, we lie and do not do what is true; but if we walk in the light as he himself is in the light, we have fellowship with one another, and the blood of Jesus his son cleanses us from all sin."

We can rejoice for the light, Jesus the Lord, is with us now, but we must "see" him and recognize his presence. The gospels tell us of our need to prepare for the Lord. We must prepare on two levels, the coming of the Lord at the end of time, but also the magnificent and many times subtle ways that God comes to us every day, through people, events, words, actions, and other assorted ways. Thus, it is proper now to cast off deeds of darkness and put on the armor of light. Jesus the light comes to dispel the darkness. It is a time to rejoice for the Lord is near!

All of us must pass through various dark nights during the journey of life. As we experience these difficult challenges we must constantly seek the light of Christ; we must respond to his call. But we know that the light is only found at the end of a tunnel. We must, therefore, persevere in order to find the light.

What dark nights have you recently experienced? How have you faired and what is your status today? For some the dark night comes in loneliness. Whether we are single, married or celibate there are times when we will be lonely. At times we think that nobody cares, not even God. For others the dark night is experienced through illness, be it our own infirmity or that of a family member or loved one. At times the tunnel begins to cave in when illness leads to death. There are times as well that the darkness is experienced through the loss of a job or underemployment, causing a financial crisis in the family. The dark night for a few is a loss of faith. We perceive the absence of God and wonder why God has abandoned us and does not answer our prayers as we think God should.

In order to successfully traverse these dark nights we must continually seek the light. The Christian journey is the movement from the darkness which is the absence of God to the birth of the light. Scripture tells us there is a need to rejoice for the light, the Lord, is always near. We can have total confidence, therefore, that whatever envelops us in darkness, whether it be loneliness, sickness or death, loss of employment, or problems with faith, it can be dispelled by our movement to the light, the prince of peace, Jesus our Lord.

The dark night of America's history in the period of slavery and Civil War was lightened by the vision and courage of Abraham Lincoln. More recently in South Africa the faith of two very different men, one a black freedom fighter, Nelson Mandela, and the second a courageous white politician, F.W. De Klerk, brought a new day to a great nation. As we travel the Christian road, let us cast off darkness and seek the light. Bathed in the presence of Jesus, we will find the proper road that leads to salvation and eternal life.

Questions To Ponder:

1. Why do I too often operate in secret, shrouded in darkness? Why am I not more transparent and seeking to radiate the light of Christ to others?

2. What is the most pervasive darkness in my life?

3. What obstacles present me from seeing the light of Christ in others, especially those with whom I might have some difficulty?

4. Why do I at times have insufficient trust that Jesus, the light, can indeed save me from the darkness of despair in my life?

5. How do I experience the light of Christ in my life?

"I am the light of the world. Whoever follows me will never walk in darkness but will have the light of life" (John 8:12).

Prayer: Lord, help me to cast off darkness and always seek the light of your truth.

Moving From Darkness To Light

Theme: Fear is an emotion that thrives on ignorance. We are instinctively afraid of what we do not know or understand. Christ has come, however, to dispel the ignorance and darkness of our life and bring us to the light of a new understanding, one based on love and sincerity. Let us cast off the ignorance that at times pervades our life and fill the void with a light of our knowledge of Christ.

Scripture To Ponder: Exodus 3:1-12; Ephesians 3:1-6; John 3:1-21

One beautiful spring morning a man went walking through his neighborhood. As he strolled along the sidewalk he noticed one of his neighbors was searching for something in the bushes that surrounded his home. "What are you looking for?" The response came, "I need to find my keys." "Where do you last remember having them?" "I had them last evening," said the neighbor, "in the basement." "Well," said the man who was walking, "why don't you look in the basement?" The answer came, "I don't want to look there; it is cold and dark." This story illustrates an important Christian theme, our need to move from the darkness of sin to the light of faith in Christ. People like to be in the light, the sunshine, but the key to life eternal begins in the darkness. Thus, it is necessary to move from darkness into light; it is necessary to respond to God's call.

The contrast between light and darkness is one of the significant themes present in the gospel of John. From the prologue to the resurrection, the author of John's gospel demonstrates the need to move from the darkness of sin to the light of Christ. Jesus is described in the prologue in these words, "The light shines in the darkness, and the darkness did not overcome it"(John 1:5). The gospel evangelist dramatically demonstrated the association of sin with darkness in describing Judas' betrayal of Jesus. When Judas left the Last Supper, the writer states, "And it was night"

(John 13:30b). Judas' great act of evil was done in darkness.

Possibly the most interesting conversion from darkness to light found in the gospel of John was the character of Nicodemus. When Nicodemus first came to Jesus he did so at night, in the darkness. Maybe this was out of fear of the Jews. Recall that Nicodemus was a Pharisee of high rank, a member of the ruling Sanhedrin or governing body of the nation. For him to be seen in the company of Jesus, whom the Jews considered to be a rebel and transgressor of the law, was to be similarly suspect in the eyes of his fellow council members. There was something about Jesus, however, that drew Nicodemus to ask him more about his message. So he came at night, secretly, in the darkness.

What was Nicodemus' initial purpose? Did he want to give Jesus some advice about how he should proceed in the future? Possibly he wanted to tell Jesus that he should be more careful, realizing that he was making many enemies among leaders of his people. Jesus' action to physically eject business people and traders from the temple was taken as an insult by many. Should he not move more slowly, more cautiously? Was it, for example wise and prudent for Jesus to defend the adulterous woman? Was it appropriate to suggest that the religious leaders had defiled the temple? Did Jesus realize that his conduct would not only raise significant notice now, but lead to the extinguishment of the light in short order?

Jesus tells Nicodemus that he knows the risks in what he does and that he understands the costs. He recounts to Nicodemus a story from their tradition about how when the Israelites were in the desert moving toward the promised land, they encountered some poisonous snakes. Moses erected an image of a serpent of bronze and raised it before them. Those who had been bitten could approach the image and find healing. Jesus recalls this image and adds, "Just as Moses lifted up the serpent in the wilderness, so must the Son of Man be lifted up, that whoever believes in him may have eternal life" (John 3: 14-15).

In other words, Jesus is telling Nicodemus that one must encounter the darkness and overcome it in order to find the light and all the beauty, power, and goodness it gives. It is clear that Nicodemus was sincere as he was fearful and worried about Jesus' welfare. But Jesus responds by challenging his visitor to move from the darkness into the light, to find the key to his own welfare in Jesus' message and with it to enter into the brightness of salvation. He calls him to be born again, to start a new life in the light of Jesus' teaching.

We are much like Nicodemus. Not only are we often in the darkness, but we need to be challenged to move into the light. We are called to look into ourselves to see the darkness there. Who of us is free of jealousy, setting double standards for ourselves and others, holding bitter memories that keep us at odds with others and more importantly darken the light of forgiveness and reconciliation? How unfortunate it is for us that we cannot simply state, "I am sorry; I was wrong."

The challenge is to identify the darkness and then to move into the light. We must begin our renewed life of faith, based not on convention but on conviction, a faith that commits itself not in terms of what we are accustomed to, but what are the highest and most significant priorities in our lives. We are challenged to develop a faith that can survive in the complex world in which we live. This faith must stand firm even in the opposition that we face from the society and cultural norms of the twenty-first-century.

Nicodemus moved from his initial darkness into light, but his conversion had only begun; his relationship with Jesus would go much further. Sometime later, when the forces of evil were beginning to surround Jesus, the Sanhedrin again met to decide his fate. The high priest at that meeting stated that those who followed Jesus were ignorant and without knowledge of the law. There is a silence; the high priest has spoken and heads nod in agreement. But the scriptures say that one man rose to his feet to present another view. Nicodemus stood in public, before those whom he was once allied and said, "Our law does not judge people without first giving them a hearing to find out what they are doing, does it?"(John 7:51). A murmur of disapproval moved through the council, but Nicodemus would not back down; he had found the light of courage. Later still when Jesus is on the cross, his body was removed by Joseph of Arimathea and placed in a tomb by Joseph and Nicodemus. Clearly, Nicodemus met the Lord Jesus in darkness and fear, but filled with courage, in the end, he responded to the call and finds the light.

Often we meet Jesus in our faith experience. We encounter him in our worship. He is present to us at such moments as the acts of kindness we experience from others as well as our own efforts at reconciliation and acts of kindness and generosity. Yet, how many of us have at times refused the joy and happiness that come from such moments and prefer the darkness of selfishness, nourished hatreds, and cultivated personal hurts? May we choose to live with courage and faith a life lived in the light which only Jesus can bring. Let us respond with generosity and open hearts to the call of the Lord this day!

Questions To Ponder:

1. What new ideas or ways of thinking frighten me? How well do I listen to the views of others with whom I disagree?

2. How much am I willing to risk in order to move from the comfort of darkness into the challenge of the light?

3. What fears hold me back from seeking the light? Why do I sometimes prefer the darkness to the light?

4. How can I bring the light of Christ to those who sit in the darkness of the secular world?

5. What manifestations of darkness must I remove from my life in order to see more clearly the light of Christ?

"The light shines in the darkness, and the darkness did not overcome it" (John 1:5).

Prayer: Lord, help me to remove the darkness of ignorance and always bask in the light of your truth.

Take A Chance On Jesus

Theme: "He who does not risk, cannot win." We have all heard this expression and while we in many ways believe it, we are too often unwilling to follow what it says. When things are fine we refuse to venture out, try new things or take a chance. We are content to stay put. This attitude, unfortunately limits our scope. Let us be open, therefore, to the possibilities others, especially Jesus, send our way.

Scripture To Ponder: Exodus 14:10-30; Acts 13:1-12; Mark 5:21-23

One day an eight-year-old boy approached an older gentleman who stood in front of a wishing well. The boy looked up and said, "I understand you are a very wise man. I would like to know the secret of life." The older man looked at the youngster and replied, "I have thought a lot in my lifetime and I believe the secret can be summed up in four words. The first thing is to think. People must think about the values by which they wish to live their life. The second idea is to believe. One must believe in oneself based on the thinking one has done about the values by which one will live his life. Third is to dream. There is a need to dream about the things that can be, based on your belief in yourself and the values upon which you plan to live your life. The last is to dare. To dare means to make your dreams become reality, based on your belief in yourself and your values." And with that, Walt Disney said to the boy, "Think, believe, dream, and dare."

The philosophy of life that Walt Disney suggested in his conversation with a young boy is based on faith, namely taking a chance on life. Others have put it this way, the one who takes no chance gains nothing. None of us will ever be able to grow and to achieve our full maturity and potential without taking any chances. To go beyond ourselves, to take a risk is somewhat challenging, because we must move beyond our own zone of comfortableness into an area that we do not know and is, therefore, uncertain. But again as the expression goes, he who does not risk cannot win.

In sports many times it's necessary to take a risk in order to defeat an opponent on the field. In business, those who are willing to risk are generally those who will move ahead. In politics, as well it may be necessary to say something that might be controversial in order to gain the advantage against a rival. While the safe course, the one most traveled by people, will generally get us where we want to go, it is the person who is able to take a reasonable chance that will gain more and find herself on top.

As taking a chance can enhance our possibilities in so many aspects of the secular world, so too can we enhance our life of faith by taking a chance on Jesus; we need to answer his call. The scriptures are filled with many examples of people who took a chance on Jesus and in the end were rewarded with the great gift they sought. Can any of us imagine the risk that was involved for those twelve apostles who answered the initial call of Jesus? Taking a chance on Jesus forced them to leave their occupations - fishing for most. For those who had them, there was a need to leave their families. We know Peter was or had been married, for the Lord cured his mother-in-law of a fever (Matthew 8:14). Not only were these men required to leave job and family, but also they were closely allied with one who was drawing lots of attention, most of it negative, from Jewish authorities. Quite clearly the apostles were required to take a great chance on Jesus, but their ability to risk provided them with the opportunity of a lifetime, to walk in the footsteps of Jesus. How many of us have dreamed of such a privilege in our life?

Many others in scripture also took a chance on Jesus. Consider the case of the Roman centurion who came to the Lord seeking a cure for his sick servant. The centurion was certainly taking a chance, not only that he would be rejected, but the significant possibility that he would be scorned and marginalized by his fellow soldiers for placing his faith in a local miracle worker from

Nazareth. Yet, Jesus praised the man, "Never have I seen such faith in all of Israel." Because he took a chance, the centurion's servant was healed. Nicodemus and Joseph of Arimathea, both upstanding members of Jewish society, took a chance on Jesus.

Nicodemus engaged the Lord in conversation so as to better understand what was necessary to find the life he sought. Later, transformed by his earlier encounter with Jesus, Nicodemus defended him against his accusers (John 7:50). Later still he and Joseph were engaged to assist with the burial of Jesus, the latter to provide a tomb and the former providing spices to anoint his body (John 19:39). The sick and marginalized of Hebrew society were willing to take a chance on Jesus. Lepers came seeking a cure; Bartimaeus called out asking for his sight. No one who took a chance on Jesus, who sought to respond to his call, was ever denied.

If we have the ability to take a chance on Jesus, to think, believe, dream, and dare, as Walt Disney would suggest, that Jesus can make a significant difference in our life, then certainly it will come true. Unfortunately, however, we live in a highly secularized world that suggests taking a chance on Jesus, an unseen God with no apparent guarantees, is a foolhardy act. Our post-enlightenment world encourages us to take a chance on the here and now; the visible is certain. Why, the world says, would one put aside a sure thing in the hopes of something that requires faith? But if Walt Disney was correct and the advice he gave to the young boy solid, then the secret of life is to look beyond the obvious, to dream, believe, think, and dare to seek other possibilities in our life. And the dreams we possess and the possibilities we dare to conceive are not restricted only to this life. Saint Paul put it well (1 Corinthians 15:19): "If for this life only we have hope in Christ, we are all people most to be pitied."

The advance of civilization in so many areas - exploration, science, medicine - as well as politics and sports, has only been achieved when people were willing to risk to go to the next level. If Columbus had never dared to sail west, how long would it have been before the New World was discovered? If Edward

Jenner had not had the courage to test his theory of inoculations, how long would it have been before a preventative medicine for smallpox was discovered? If Abraham Lincoln had not tested the political waters in 1860 against better known and more qualified opponents, who would have had the courage to end slavery?

In a similar sense, in order to answer his call, we must be willing to take a chance on Jesus. Faith today is countercultural, but the Christian life if well led will always be a bit unpopular. Jesus did not promise us popularity or an easy and safe road, but he did promise life eternal to those who took the narrow path. Let us listen to Jesus, follow the philosophy of Walt Disney and never fail to think, believe, dream, and dare as Christians. The reward will be eternal life.

Questions To Ponder:

1. When was the last time I took a chance on another person, especially an individual others have cast aside?

2. What happened to the basic faith that always placed my trust in the Lord, believing that in the end, all will be well?

3. What do I need to do to cast out fear in my life? What has happened to my trust in others and God?

4. What am I willing to risk of the goods in this temporal world in order to find the gift of eternal life with God?

5. To what degree do I actually believe, dream and dare? Why am I at times so timid?

"Ask, and it will be given you; search and you will find; knock, and the door will be opened for you" (Luke 11:9).

Prayer: Lord Jesus, help me to believe in possibilities, things beyond my immediate purview.

Keep Your Eye On The Goal!

Theme: From our youth to the end of our life, we are constantly setting goals. They may be an education, athletics, business or some personal endeavor. Experience teaches us that we must keep our eyes fixed on the goals in order to achieve them. Such is the case in our ultimate goal of life, namely finding eternal life with Christ. We must keep our eyes on the great prize.

Scripture To Ponder: Genesis 12:1-9; 1 Peter 1:16-21; Matthew 7:7-11

In the days of the great sailing ships, it was common for the captain to hire a few young men who would serve as cabin boys during the voyage. One of the tasks of these cabin boys was to periodically climb the mainmast to the top crows' nest so that he could serve as a lookout when the ship approached land or if there was some need to observe the distant horizon. Often when these young lads began their ascent of the mainmast they made the mistake of looking down. When they did so, the height, combined with the periodic rocking of the ship, made the lads dizzy, too often leading them to fall and either be severely injured or die. Thus, they were always instructed by some of the older crew members that when they made their ascent they were to always keep their eye on the crows' nest, the goal which they sought.

Keeping one's eye on the goal was not only good advice for cabin boys; it has been and always will be solid instruction in living the Christian life. Salvation history is essentially the story of how God instructed the Jews and their ancestors in faith, the Christians, to keep their eyes on the goal, namely maintenance of their relationship with God. The scriptures contain numerous examples of those who successfully kept their eyes on the goal and, in the end, achieved their desired end.

Abraham and Moses were asked by God to take on significant tasks and they completed them successfully by keeping their eyes fixed on the goal. Abram, we are told, was a wandering Aramean, a nomad from the land of Ur (Genesis 11:27-12:9). God's plan of salvation began in earnest way when he came to Abram and asked him to journey to an unknown land. He was told that he would be the father of a great nation, yet he and his wife, Sarah, were older, not, at least in normal circumstances, at the age to conceive and bear children. Despite the uncertainty of responding to an unknown God, Abram, whose name was expanded to Abraham, kept his eye on the goal, doing whatever was asked. He was even willing to sacrifice his son, Isaac, his one chance of progeny (Genesis 22:1-14). By keeping his eye on the goal he became the first great patriarch and the father of a great nation, as God had promised.

Hundreds of years later Moses was also given a Herculean task. Called by God in the desert, in the form of a burning bush that was not consumed (Exodus 3:1-22), Moses was asked to lead the Israelites back to their homeland. The task was anything but easy. He had to deal with the stubbornness of Pharaoh and possibly even more distressing the frequent complaints from his own people as they wandered rather aimlessly, due to their disobedience, spending forty years in transit to the promised land. Yet, despite the many forces arrayed against him, Moses kept his eyes firmly fixed on the goal and, like Abraham, achieved his end.

Unfortunately, the Hebrew Bible also narrates the failures of many leaders in Israel to keep their eyes on the goal, leading to disaster for the Jewish community. After God destroyed all their enemies and the people were settled in their tribes in the promised land, infidelity to God and his commandments began almost immediately. The people turned away from God, which led to their destruction at the hands of their enemies. God sent judges, such as Gideon, Deborah, and Samson to rescue the people and for a short time they returned to God. In the end, however, they continued to fall away from their goal.

After the establishment of the monarchy and the reigns of David and Solomon, the rulers of the northern kingdom of Israel and the southern kingdom of Judah lost their vision and worshiped false gods, as well as mistreating the most vulnerable within Hebrew society. God's displeasure with these rulers led to the destruction of the northern kingdom by the Assyrians and the exile of Judah to Babylon for fifty years. Failure to keep their eye on the goal thus brought much pain and even destruction and death to the Hebrews.

The inability of those placed in positions of authority in ancient Israel to maintain their attention on their ultimate goal must be contrasted with the absolute obedience and direction of Jesus Christ. Jesus kept himself focused on the goal and never considered the price he would pay. Jesus' call to the apostles must indeed have been strong for we are told that they "immediately" left their livelihood and family to be his followers.

Yet, these first followers came to realize that their discipleship required them, like their master, to keep their eyes fixed on the goal. It would not be an easy road. On the contrary, Jesus warned his followers: "I am sending you out like lambs into the midst of wolves" (Luke 10:3). But then Jesus pointed them toward the proper path to achieve their goal: "Enter through the narrow gate; for the gate is wide and the road is easy that leads to destruction, and there are many who take it. For the gate is narrow and the road is hard that leads to life, and there are few who find it" (Matthew 7:13-14).

Jesus called his disciples to be dedicated; he challenged them to keep their eyes on the goal. On one occasion Jesus told a band of would-be followers that their discipleship must be complete. He asked one person to follow, but the individual asked permission to bury his dead father. Jesus responded, "Let the dead bury their own dead; but as for you go and proclaim the kingdom of God" (Matthew 8:22). Another said he would follow, but asked permission to bid farewell to his family. Jesus told that man, "No one who puts hand to the plow and looks back is fit for the kingdom of God" (Luke 9: 59-62).

People today might feel that Jesus' reaction was rather harsh, but he was only describing the need for complete dedication to purpose; he was asking his followers to keep their eyes on the goal. The Lord put it very directly when he said, "If any want to become my followers, let them deny themselves and take up their cross and follow me. For those who want to save their life will lose it, and those who lose their life for my sake will find it" (Matthew 16: 24b-25).

Jesus' demands for his followers were exemplified in his own life. Whatever the goal was, whether short-term or longer, Jesus never flinched from moving forward and doing what was necessary. He was not deterred from curing people on the sabbath, even though the law said such action was forbidden. He did not refrain from speaking his mind, whether that was in the synagogue in Nazareth, conversations with the Scribes and Pharisees, or chastising Peter, his personal choice to lead the nascent Christian community. He did not avoid conflict; he never "sugar-coated" his message, that the road would be difficult and priorities must be straight.

Jesus was very clear in telling his disciples: "Whoever loves father or mother more than me is not worthy of me; and whoever loves son or daughter more than me is not worthy of me; and whoever does not take up the cross and follow me is not worthy of me" (Luke 10:37-38). Jesus never shied away from doing what was difficult, whether it was overturning the tables of the money changers in the temple, or courageously walking the Via Dolorosa to his own ignominious death.

The challenge Jesus gave to his first followers is still present in the twenty-first century. In fact, in some ways the trial may be greater. Our ultimate goal, whether we think about it or not on a daily basis, is to return home to God. That long-term goal is achieved by shorter-term objectives, each of which requires our attention and focus. The allurements of contemporary society, whether they are the generic ideas of secularism and relativism or the more specific things of materialism, power, and prestige seek, almost on a daily basis, to derail us from moving in a clear and positive direction toward our goals. Thus, we must not look down, as the experienced sailors taught the young cabin boy when climbing to the crows' nest, but rather look up and keep our eyes set on the goal. We may feel left aside by contemporary society, but our goal is not in this world, but rather an eternal existence with God, the one from whom we came. Therefore, let us keep our eyes clearly fixed on the goal; the rewards may not be as plentiful today, but they will be found in the eternal life to come.

Questions To Ponder:

1. How much do I allow the allurements of the world to cloud my vision of the goal of building God's kingdom in this world?

2. What criteria do I use when setting goals in my life?

3. What are my priorities in my day-to-day life? Why do I allow the world to at times trump my need for God?

4. Do I keep my eyes set on the goal of eternal life or do the allurements of the world present too much of a temptation?

5. What is the principle temptation or object of our life that competes with my goal of finding eternal life with Christ?

"One does not live by bread alone, but by every word that comes from the mouth of God" (Matthew 4:4b).

Prayer: Lord, let me never be discouraged by lack of result, but keep my resolve clear and true in always following you.

Finding The Lost

Theme: Prejudice, the act of pre-judging people, is unfortunately rather rampant in our society. As Christians, however, we are called to take the non-prejudicial method of Jesus in reaching out to all, but especially those who stand on the margins of our society.

Scripture To Ponder: Wisdom 11:22-12:1; 2 Thessalonians 1:11-2:2; Luke 19: 1-10

Baseball fans today might not recall the name Branch Rickey, but for what he did for America's national pastime, he should not only be well known but enshrined in a place of honor. Rickey was raised in Ohio in a family with a strict Protestant moral ethic. He understood the value of people and the equality each person had in the eyes of God. This fundamental belief and his consequent pioneering efforts on the behalf of the "lost" would bring him to baseball's coveted Hall of Fame.

Branch Rickey played baseball in college and was good enough to play a few years professionally, but his great claim to fame came not on the field but in the front office of major league baseball. After his brief stint on the field, he managed the Saint Louis Cardinals for a few years in the 1920s, but then he moved into the front office as president and general manager of the team. His wise decision making transformed Saint Louis from a team that was second rate to a World Series champion. In fact, St. Louis won the series three times during his over twenty years with the team, as manager or executive.

In 1942, however, Rickey moved east to Brooklyn to take up the general manager position with the Dodgers. Always looking for good talent and ever cognizant of his strong belief in equality of all human beings, Rickey heard about a fabulous athlete who was attending UCLA. His name was Jackie Robinson. Robinson was an athlete who could do it all, but his great forte was track and field. Nonetheless, Rickey spoke to Robinson and asked him if he was interested in playing major league baseball. There was only one major problem - Robinson was African-American and there had never been a black player in the major leagues. Robinson agreed to Rickey's terms. Basically, Rickey asked the young athlete to ignore the slurs, inappropriate actions, and general rejection that was certain to come when he, an African-American, would step on the diamond of a major league field. When Jackie Robinson joined the Dodgers in 1947 all that Rickey anticipated came true, but Robinson was up to the test. He proved his mettle beyond expectation, playing for ten years with distinction. He was voted rookie of the year in 1947 and most valuable player in 1949; he was six times selected to the National League All-Star team.

In 1955, Branch Rickey moved again, this time to Pittsburgh to another front office job. While the Pirates as a team did not markedly improve under his direction, he again took the bold step of reaching out to another "lost" group who had previously been ignored by major league baseball. In 1955, he recruited and signed Roberto Clemente, who became the first Hispanic player in the major leagues. Like Robinson ten years earlier, Clemente was a star and paved the way for so many others to follow.

Branch Rickey took a chance and went out on a limb, to bring to prominence people who had been placed on the margins simply because of the color of their skin or their ethnic background. Scripture speaks of how Jesus reached out to those on the margins, demonstrating his total inclusivity. The Lord's search for those who are lost serves as a challenge for us to respond to his call and to do our part to speak out on behalf of others in imitation of Jesus, the one in whose footsteps we wish to walk.

Saint Luke (19:1-10) told the story of Zacchaeus, one who from a Jewish perspective was lost, and his encounter with Jesus. A tax collector, like Matthew, Zacchaeus would have been placed on the margins by Hebrew society, but Jesus noticed him as he entered Jericho and in a public way brings him into Jesus' fold. Certainly those observing the scene must have been shocked that

Jesus invited himself to the home of the tax collector for meal. Why would this man, who claimed to be so close to God and did such miraculous works, intentionally associate with someone who was hated, a nobody in Jewish society, a person who had lost his way? Clearly, Jesus was trying to teach a lesson that God's message goes out to all people; no one is excluded. Jesus was preaching a message of inclusivity; he was reversing the conventional wisdom of the day. As Jesus said, "The Son of Man came to seek out and to save the lost" (Luke 19:10).

Jesus' outreach to the marginalized was demonstrated on numerous other occasions. He intentionally reached out to lepers (Matthew 8:1-4), allowed a hemorrhaging woman to touch him (Mark 5:25-34), engaged the Samaritan woman in conversation (John 4:7-30) and fearlessly cast out many demons from Legion (Mark 5:1-20). He was not afraid to support the woman caught in the act of adultery (John 8:2-11) and accepted the invitation of Matthew to dinner (Matthew 9:9-13).

Actually, however, Jesus' actions should not have been that unexpected. The book of Wisdom (11:22 - 12:18) clearly says that God's mercy, compassion, and concern goes out to all. God rejects no one, for he is the Creator of all. Since God wills that things exist, it is impossible that he would do anything other than preserve what he created. These words, applied to Zacchaeus, suggest the reason Jesus overtly sought him out and made him an example for all who observed these events. The message was clear: God looks for and rescues the lost.

Jesus' outreach to Zacchaeus, a manifestation of God's preservation of life, impacts us in two significant ways. First, the Lord's action gives us reason for hope in our lives. There are times when we are lost, when our natural and proper direction toward God is thrown out of whack and we move in ways which may even be directly opposed to God. Since we are the creation of God, we can take solace in the fact that the Lord will never abandon us, but rather, using the image of Francis Thompson's epic poem, *The Hound of Heaven*, we know that God leaves no stone unturned in a diligent search for us.

This should be a great consolation when we realize we have gone astray. But Jesus' action with a tax collector also challenges us to respond to his call and then follow his example. Too often we reject individuals or groups for many varied, but seldom proper, reasons. Many members of society today are lost, stand on the margins, and are not allowed to participate fully. In the time of Branch Rickey, as hard as it might be to conceive today, black and hispanic athletes were not allowed to participate in professional sports. They were lost, but through persistence, they were found through the efforts of one courageous man. We must be like Branch Rickey, respond to Jesus' call, seek out the lost of our society, and bring them to the fold as did Jesus in his outreach to Zacchaeus. Let us be aware that God will find us and we must have the courage to seek and to find others, to the glory and praise of God.

Questions To Ponder:

1. Why am I too timid in responding to Jesus' call? Can I reach out more boldly to those who are lost?

2. Who are the lost people in society to whom I must respond?

3. When was the last time I overtly went out of my way to meet the needs of a person who stands on the margins - the poor, handicapped, and the disenfranchised?

4. What do I need to do in my life to be more accepting of those who are different then me?

5. When was the last time I shared my faith with a person who has lost their Christian identity and become more attached to the world than to God?

"For whoever does the will of my Father in heaven is my brother and sister and mother" (Matthew 12:50).

Prayer: Lord Jesus, help me to respond to the needs of my brothers and sisters, and not count the cost.

Seeking God Before All Else

Theme: The busyness of the twenty-first-century in which we live at times leads us to compromise our priorities. We know in our heart that God must always be the first priority, but the enticements of the world and the responsibilities we hold sometimes cloud our vision. We must return to our roots and realize that if we seek God first all else will be given to us.

Scripture To Ponder: 1 Kings 3:5-12; Romans 8:28-30; Matthew 13:44-52

"Late have I loved you, O Beauty so ancient and so new, late have I loved you." This famous line comes from Saint Augustine's equally famous autobiography, *The Confessions.* It was written after a life of trial and searching, leading to conversion and the discovery of God. Augustine was born in the city of Thagaste, now in the country of Algeria, in the year 354. His father, Patricius, was a Roman citizen and pagan; his mother, Monica, was a prayerful Christian woman. As a youth he was an intelligent, questioning boy. Yet, he seemed to live his life as an individual; he was quite self-centered. All of life was for him: his projects, his education, his welfare. As a young man he became a teacher of rhetoric and was well known for his intelligence and probing mind.

Despite his fame and success, his life of "individualism" lacked something. The void he felt was community; he needed the presence of others and he needed God. Thus, he began to search for that which was missing in his life. Pagan religions offered nothing to this man of intellect. Manichaeism, a semi-Christian dualistic philosophy, attracted him for a short while, but after a few years he found this empty and hollow as well. Finally he answered the call to Christianity. He found people; he found community. He found God. He learned that the world was not me; the world is us!

Saint Augustine's life of searching and conversion illustrates a central message of scripture, namely that we must be willing to give up all in order to seek and find the greatest of all gifts - Jesus Christ. In 1 Kings 3:5-12, God gave Solomon the chance of a lifetime. The Lord said he could choose one gift from God. Solomon was given the proverbial genie in the bottle option.

We have all heard tales of the stranger marooned on a desert isle who finds an old and ornate bottle, opens same and out pops a genie, ready to grant the stranger one wish. God is not a genie, but the choice he gave to Solomon was just as tempting. Solomon could have had anything, and thus, many might view his choice as rather odd. It seems that Solomon chose for others in choosing wisdom over personal wants and desires, but what he actually did was choose God. He chose a gift that would make him better able to serve his people and, therefore, to do what God asked of him. Solomon had his priorities clear and in order. He was willing to forego personal ambition, achievement, and material gain in order to choose the higher gift, the presence of God in his life.

Certainly this is the message of the three short parables that Jesus proposed in Matthew 13:44-52. Jesus suggested that we must be like the owner of the field and the pearl merchant who were both willing to sell all they had in order to possess the great treasure or the pearl of great price. But there was possibly an even greater challenge in the parable of the dragnet in the lake. We are asked to set aside all those things in our life that are so tempting, but are ultimately useless in our quest to find Christ. We get rather attached to the creature comforts of our world, and thus, we don't readily divest ourselves of these items. We are asked to be like the wise and learned scribe who knows the difference between what is old and new, that is what gives life and what does not.

Are we willing to sell all in order to find the great gifts of Jesus and salvation? Do we realize that we, like Augustine, need to be converted? Do we realize that at times we come late to the game — yes, late have we loved Christ, who is ever ancient, yet ever new? We need to take stock of the various ways our priorities become askew and how the things that are really not that important get ahead of our relationship with Christ.

In business we might use tactics or methods that are unethical, skirt about others, or simply ignore problems with the hope they won't show up later. Do we sell our integrity for the company? Many of us place personal accomplishment and achievement ahead of God. For some, the need to accomplish academic goals forces us to ignore God. How often has one heard, "Oh, I can't go to church this Sunday; I have other things that are more important." Students too often do not realize that the time spent before the television could have been better spent with God. Young people involved with sports have the same challenge. We hear: I can't miss practice or the game; my coach will not understand. But if I fail to go to church, God will understand. Leisure and pleasure often come before God; we won't sell or give away one moment of our precious free time for God. Too often today when we go on vacation, we take a break from God as well. Yes, often it is true, "Late have we loved God."

Sometimes we get off stride and our priorities are compromised, but there is a solution. God will provide for all our needs, but we must be confident that, if we do let go, God will assist us. Paul told the Romans (8:28): "We know that all things work together for good for those who love God, who are called according to his purpose." This must be our consolation and our joy.

Augustine was a great saint, but he needed to be converted to his need for Christ. Once he found the path, however, nothing stopped him in his quest to fulfill God's will in his life. Inspired by Augustine, confident that God is with us, and strengthened by the word of God, let us go forward, sell all and find God; the reward will be eternal life.

Questions To Ponder:

1. How much time do I spend seeking the things of God as opposed to the things of the world?

2. How do I set my daily priorities? Where in this list of "things to do" is the task to improve my relationship with Jesus?

3. What do I need to do to make my Christian vision clearer?

4. What might I need to lessen or eliminate in my life in order to more fully and clearly listen to and carry out the message of the gospel?

5. If asked by God for one wish, what would it be? Why?

"Seek the Lord and live" (Amos 5:6).

Prayer: Lord, help me to find you, knowing then I have found my way.

Answering God's Call

Theme: Challenges in life come in many varied ways. We find challenges at home, at work, in our local communities and even in our churches. When we feel comfortable we answer the call, but often when the summons is a challenge we are hesitant or falter. God is constantly calling us to renew and enhance our relationship with him. Let us answer the call.

Scripture to Ponder: Jeremiah 20:10-13; Romans 5:12-15; Matthew 10:26-33

William Jennings Bryan, one of the most famous political figures in American history, yet little known today, was truly a man who answered the call. Bryan was born in 1860 at the dawn of the Civil War in Salem, Illinois. He received his education at Illinois College and Union College of Law in Chicago and began practicing in 1883. He moved to Nebraska and became very popular with local people in Lincoln as an advocate for those with little or no voice in society. Content to continue his law practice, Bryan was convinced by local citizens to run for congress; he was elected and served two terms from 1892-1896. He was a great proponent of the Populist cause of coinage of silver and gold as a solution to the economic depression which struck the United States in 1893.

His famous "Cross of Gold" speech, supporting bimetallism, delivered at the 1896 Democratic National Convention, was so persuasive that at the young age of 36, he was nominated to run for president. He lost that election to the Republican William McKinley, but he continued to answer the call. Four years later, the Democrats again asked him to run and again he lost.

Despite his failure to win the presidency, the fame of William Jennings Bryan grew through his great speeches and oratorical style which became legendary. He traveled throughout the nation to promote the policies for which he stood. In 1901, Bryan founded the *Commoner*, a weekly newspaper published that advocated progressive political causes. In 1908, the Democrats asked their champion to run for president a third time. The result was a third loss, this time to William Howard Taft. Defeat could not dissuade Bryan from assisting others in need and thus he accepted President Woodrow Wilson's invitation to serve as Secretary of State. He served with distinction from 1913 to 1915, but after the United States became hostile toward Germany he resigned under protest, believing the administration's action to be immoral. He was the champion of many popular causes, leading the fight for the popular election of United States senators and standing at the forefront of the women's suffrage issue which culminated in the nineteenth amendment to the Constitution. Bryan was also active in the temperance movement and fought for prohibition.

The final episode of his life quite possibly is the one for which he will be most remembered. In 1925, Bryan again answered the call, this time he was asked to leave retirement one last time and be the champion of religion in the famous 1925 Scopes "Monkey" trial in Dayton, Tennessee. John Scopes, a high school biology teacher, was accused of teaching the scientific theory of evolution in his classroom, a practice that was against the state law passed that very year. Bryan was counsel for the prosecution, defending the fundamentalist Protestant cause. Clarence Darrow, the famous jurist from Chicago, was Scopes' defense counsel. The famous play and equally popular movie *Inherit the Wind* tells the story of this famous trial. Scopes was convicted; Darrow had been defeated. William Jennings Bryan had earned his last hurrah; he died one week after the trial ended. He was a man who, to the very end, answered the call.

God, from the dawn of human civilization has been asking his people to answer the call. Salvation history is replete with stories of people who were asked to do difficult tasks, many of which they did not want to do, in response to the call of the Lord. Noah built the ark to save his family and preserve humanity and God's creation of the animal kingdom. Abraham left his homeland, went to a foreign place at the request of the Lord, and now we honor him as the father of a great nation, the Hebrew people. Moses led the Israelites out of bondage in Egypt; many judges answered God's call to rally Israel at a time of national need.

The prophets also answered the call of the Lord, even when they believed themselves not qualified for the job. Jeremiah was only a youth and ill-prepared, but God told him, "Before I formed you in the womb I knew you, and before you were born I consecrated you; I appointed you a prophet to the nations." Even though the prophet worried about his youth, God responded, "Do not say, 'I am only a boy'; for you shall go to all to whom I send you. Do not be afraid of them. For I am with you to deliver you" (Jeremiah 1:5-7). We recall how Amos (7:14-15) did not want the task God gave him: "I am no prophet, nor a prophet's son; but I am a herdsman, and a dresser of sycamore trees, and the Lord took me from following the flock, and the Lord said to me, 'Go, prophesy to my people.'" In all of these cases God asked something difficult, time consuming, and possibly fear-filled of men who considered themselves ordinary, unqualified, and simply not right for the job. Yet, in faith they all answered God's call and in the process wrote chapters in the great account of salvation history.

Jesus of Nazareth chose twelve unlearned, rather ordinary men, at least in all the ways people today would judge qualifications, for a very difficult task. He called these men, fishermen for the most part, one-by-one to join his mission, and they all said "yes" without hesitation. These men had no idea what the call would entail, but they joined nonetheless, so impressive and powerful was the call of the Lord. At first the call was passive; all that the apostles were required to do was walk with the Lord and listen to his words. But then Jesus added more to the stakes; the call became active when he sent them out, two-by-two on mission to do the Lord's work. They went without staff, money, change of clothes, or food. In other words, they went forth in faith that all that would be necessary for the task would be provided. They were to preach the good news, effect cures, and lead people to Jesus. They obviously did their work very well; the church today exists because of their efforts.

We have all been called individually by name and collectively by community to answer God's call. The call first came at baptism. Our name was announced to all the Christian community that day; we became members of this special body of faith which we call the church. We were called that day, although we most probably did not realize it, to service, to ministry, to an active pursuit of God. We live that call as a community. The community needs our input. If we sit around and do nothing, allowing everyone else to do what is necessary, then we have missed the call. In the process we have missed the opportunity of a lifetime to show the face of Christ to others.

What exactly is the call that all Christians are challenged to answer? It is the call of the prophets and the apostles; it is a call to proclaim God's message of peace by all that we say and do. It is the call to live in a way others would wish to emulate. It is the call to do what God asks of us, at all times and be joyful in our actions. This, quite obviously, is not a simple task. That is why it is necessary that all of us be involved, in some way, in going forth to actively answer God's call.

We can answer the call of God in many ways. Each person must determine what the answer will be. Whatever the answer, it must be an active participation! Like the patriarchs and prophets we may not think ourselves qualified; we may not want the job. But we must answer God's call, as freely and immediately as did the apostles, for our benefit now and for the needs of our world. We must answer the call to make the kingdom come, now and to eternal life.

Answering the call of the Lord has always been a great challenge and so it is today. There will be many obstacles that society will throw into our path. We may be ridiculed by friends and colleagues for the words we say and the actions we perform; we may feel unqualified for the task, submit to laziness or cowardice, or simply not want to participate. Answering

God's call will not always be fun, but many of the greatest accomplishments and, thereby satisfactions, in life have been done through challenge. Thus, while it is important to always try and find the bright side of every event and discover the good in every action, the reality is that many things we are asked to do by God will not be pleasant. It is generally not fun to visit a sick relative, neighbor, or business associate in the hospital, but to do so means answering God's call. It is difficult and not fun for parents to discipline their children, to provide them with "tough love" when enabling another is much simpler, but that is answering God's call. It isn't easy to take the ethical way in work practices when we are pressured to take short cuts that might hurt another or be unfair, but that is answering God's call.

God is calling, are we answering? Go, Jesus says, preach the good news, heal the sick, help others. The road of discipleship will be filled with many potholes, twisting turns, and obstacles, but we can and must go forward with faith. Why? We have God's promise of success: "Know that I am with you always, until the end of the world" (Matthew 28:20b).

Questions To Ponder:

1. When God calls me to action, especially when it is immediate or unexpected, how have I answered this summons to action?

2. Why do I shy away or refuse to engage challenging situations? Why does my faith in such circumstances falter?

3. What important lessons have I learned from the great challenges in my life?

4. Why do I sometimes fail to listen to the call the Lord; why am I so closed minded?

5. What new challenge has the Lord placed before me?

"Immediately they [Peter and Andrew] left and their father and followed him." (Matthew 4:22).

Prayer: God, our Father, help me to hear your call and grant me the grace to say "yes."

Finding Jesus In All Things

Theme: The darkness that too often clouds our world can, if we are not careful, convince us that God is absent. However, our faith teaches us and we know in our hearts that God is ever present. Thus, it is a challenge to find God, especially in those people, events, and situations we find most difficult and troubling. Let us seek God every day in all we do and say.

Scripture To Ponder: 1 Samuel 3:1-10; Galatians 1:11-24; Matthew 4:18-22

A man and his young son went on a camping trip to the mountains. They hired an experienced guide who brought them into the heart of a great forest, and the beauty spots in the mountains that they themselves would never have found. The guide was forever pointing out beauty and wonders that the mere passer-by would never notice. The young boy was fascinated by the ability of the guide to see so much in the surroundings. As they walked, the young lad was so impressed that he exclaimed, "I will bet you can see God out here." The guide smiled and replied, "Son, as life goes on, it is getting hard for me to see anything but God out here."

As the story suggests, generally speaking, people expect to find God in the grand and glorious, the great and the stereotypically obvious places. These might include a church, sacred shrine, sacraments, such as a cross, icon, a person of known spirituality or holiness, the Bible or other religious texts. However, an examination of scripture shows us that while God can certainly be found in the so-called "obvious" places or people, the Lord is also present in the subtle and less obvious places and individuals as well. The Hebrew Bible certainly describes God's presence in powerful events. The great flood described in the book of Genesis, the ten plagues wrought against Pharaoh and the Egyptian people, the Israelites' passage through the Red Sea, and the destruction of Jericho, are examples of the powerful presence of God. Yet, God is equally and possibly even more remarkably present in more subtle and unexpected events.

Elijah was told by God to wait at the mouth of the cave and the Lord would pass by. The great prophet experienced an earthquake, fire, and strong wind, yet God was not present in any of these "expected" manifestations. God instead was found in the soft gentle breeze. Naaman, the Syrian, a king but a leper, sought the assistance of Elisha to be cured of his affliction in some miraculous way. He reacted quite negatively when told simply to go wash seven times in the Jordan River. Yet, in the simplicity of such an action, God was found and he was cured (2 Kings 5:1-19a).

The subtle touch of God was also found in the call of the prophets. Amos (7:4) describes himself as a shepherd and a dresser of sycamores, yet God called him to preach a message of social justice to the northern kingdom of Israel. Isaiah (6:8c), writing to the southern kingdom of Judah prior to the exile was surprised by the call of God yet forcefully proclaimed, "Here am I; send me!"

In a similar way, Jesus demonstrated power that clearly marked him as God, but he was also subtle, demonstrating that God can be found in all things. The numerous miracle stories of Jesus, curing people and raising others from the dead mark him as God. The apostles were convinced of Jesus' divinity when he calmed the storm on the Sea of Galilee (Mark 4:35-41). The Transfiguration, narrated by all three synoptic evangelists (Matthew 17:1-8; Mark 9:2-8; Luke 9:28-36), was another clear indication of Jesus' divinity. But Jesus' presence was found in much more subtle ways as well. His call of the apostles was simple and straightforward. With no outward show of power, Jesus asked Peter and Andrew and then a moment later, James and John to follow him. We are told that they "immediately" left their livelihood and their families to become his followers. Clearly, these men could find God in the subtlety of Jesus' call.

Where do we find God? We expect to find the Lord in certain places and people. The privilege we possess of the church, the sacraments, the saints, and the scriptures allows most people to find God rather easily. We have no problems discovering God in people we love and those with whom we choose to associate. The great challenge is to find God in the places, events, situations, and most importantly people who create challenges for us in this life. Events of great sadness or tragedy, those of defeat, incidents of physical or psychological pain are not where we would expect to find God.

Yet, if we reflect on past events that at the time seemed so void of God, we can, in most cases, find God in what transpired. Surely death, destruction, or financial ruin are things we would always seek to avoid, yet in the mystery of God's providence, the Lord is present even there. On the journey of life, situations arise which again challenge our sensibility of God's presence. How, we ask, could God possibly be present when infidelity leads to the destruction of relationships or loss of financial security forces us to radically shift our style of life, where we live and the things that we can do? We are at a loss to find God in those people who create mayhem for others, destroy the credibility of institutions, stand on the opposite side than us on key social and political issues, or have hurt us in some way.

One of the great challenges of Christianity is to discover the presence of God where we do not expect the Lord to be. The little boy's unexpected question arose from his innocence and lack of inhibition, but somehow he was prompted to see God present all around him. Yes, life forces us to take many detours, and we find many bumps and roadblocks along the way, yet even in these "darker hours" of our lives, the presence of God must be found. God has a plan for each of his children that plays out in our day-to-day lives. Yet, as they say, God writes straight with crooked lines. Our life is not a linear progression from point A to point B; rather we take a complicated and circuitous route, but God is present at every turn.

The famous Trappist monk and spiritual writer Thomas Merton in his popular autobiography *The Seven Story Mountain*, expressed in a beautiful way the quest to find God in all things: "In one sense we are always traveling, and traveling as if we did not know where we were going. In another sense we have already arrived. We cannot arrive at the perfect possession of God in this life, and that is why we are traveling and in darkness. But we already possess him by grace, and therefore, in that sense, we have arrived at our dwelling in the light. But oh! How far have I to go to find you in whom I have already arrived!" Yes, God is ever present let us open our eyes to see him and our arms to welcome him.

Questions To Ponder:

1. Why do I seek Jesus only in the obvious places and triumphant events of my life? What must I do to find him in the mundane and problematic as well?

2. What situations or events do I find most problematic in finding God? Why?

3. When was the last time I went out of my way to find the presence of God in a person whom I find difficult?

4. How can I transform difficult situations and events, where God seems to be absent, into situations in which God can and must be found?

5. What needs to be transformed or changed in me to be able to find the presence of God on a daily basis?

"Seek the Lord while he may be found, call upon him while he is near" (Isaiah 55:6).

Prayer: Lord, help me to find you in all people, but especially the poor and marginalized.

Section III

Placing Our Hope and Trust in Jesus

Introduction

A team of world famous botanists was in the Amazon rain forest searching for and cataloging rare or possibly never discovered plants. The leader of the group, using high-powered binoculars, searched into a deep canyon and spotted a flower, which from his memory and expertise, had never been discovered or catalogued. The problem, however, was how to get down to this particular location. As it turned out, there was a young lad from a small village in the general area who was observing the work of the scientists. The leader of the group went to the young lad and said, "I will give you twenty dollars if you will go over the side of this ledge on a rope and obtain for us a flower I have discovered."

The young lad looked over the situation and responded, "I can help, but please give me a few minutes and I will return." As he promised, the young lad returned in about five minutes with an older man. The young lad spoke again, "I will go over the ledge and retrieve the flower for you, as long as this man holds the rope. He is my father."

The little story begs the question, whom do you trust? Can we place our trust in the world, friends, family, our biological parents or our Father in heaven? Contemporary life suggests that we should place our hope and trust in the physical world in which we live. We are told to trust the government as an entity that not only oversees its citizens, but cares for them. It is suggested that we trust the economy, believing that our capitalist system works well for the betterment of all people. We are asked to trust business, accepting that companies and those who run them are fair and honest, seeking the common good. We are almost forced to trust in professionals such as physicians, attorneys, tax consultants, and the like because we do not have the expertise they possess.

In all these cases, however, we all know that far too often the trust we place in people and institutions is misguided. We are often disappointed and possibly even harmed by the trust we place in the world and its various institutions and peoples. It is natural for humans to reach out to that which is visible, tangible, and readily accessible. Yet, the only sure bet when it comes to trust is to place our confidence in God. As the book of Proverbs (3:5) states, "Trust in the Lord with all your heart, and do not rely on your own insight."

God can be trusted, but sometimes this reality needs to be re-cemented in our minds. Trust is clearly the central virtue; we must trust God in order to walk in the footsteps of Jesus. Trusting God requires persistence; we can never give up realizing that God's plan and timetable are seldom our own. Thus, we patiently place our trust in the Lord. Trust also necessitates that we surrender ourselves to the power and presence of God. There is no need to demonstrate strength, but rather to trust that God's strength and power will suffice for all our needs. Trust requires us to place total reliance on God for what we need. This is indeed difficult since our visible manifestations of God are not always obvious. Still, such trust is absolutely necessary in order to walk with Jesus. Trust also challenges us to believe that nothing is too complex for God. If we cast out fear then we can enter through the narrow gate of eternal life. Let us, therefore, continue our quest to walk in the footsteps of Jesus by placing our hope and trust in him.

Trust, The Central Virtue

Theme: We have often heard and sometimes said, "If you want to get the job done do-it-yourself." Such a comment reflects a lack of trust in others. The manifestations of our inability to trust are numerous and they impact family, coworkers and even God. Trust is a virtue we need to develop more fully. It will help release us from our need to control everything. Trust brings us closer to others and most importantly, to God.

Scriptures To Ponder: Acts 2:42-47; 1 Peter 1:3-9; John 20:19-31

One Saturday night, a newly ordained minister received a last-minute assignment from his bishop to deliver the Sunday sermon at the bishop's church. The young minister asked, "Bishop, how can I do this with such little notice? I have never preached before a large congregation such as yours and I have nothing prepared." The bishop simply replied, "Trust the Lord, young man. Just trust the Lord." Later that night, the young minister, searching for an idea for his homily, was seeking inspiration from the Bible.

As he flipped through the pages of a Bible which was in the bishop's office, he came upon some typewritten notes that were tucked away in the pages. After reading them over, he liked them so much he decided to use them in the pulpit the next morning. With the notes before him, the young man made a splendid debut before the cathedral congregation. Many spoke positively about his homily, stating that what he said was filled with wisdom beyond his years. As they filed out of the church, many parishioners complimented the young minister for his excellent preaching. At the end of the line came the bishop. He said, "Young man, you preached the sermon I was going to deliver today. Those were my notes. What shall I do?" The young minister responded, "Trust the Lord, Bishop. Trust the Lord."

The bishop received a "dose of his own medicine" when the young minister challenged him to trust in God. In a similar way, Christians today must demonstrate greater trust, in ourselves, in others, and most especially in God. Scripture provides significant insight into this necessity.

The first half of the Acts of the Apostles chronicles the activity of the early church during those first days after Jesus' ascension. Luke, the author, showed how those first followers of Jesus exhibited complete trust in each other and in the Lord. Rather than watching out only for their own needs and being concerned with their own material possessions, these people willingly devoted themselves to each other by placing complete trust in the community. Luke wrote, "All who believed were together and had all things in common; they would sell their possessions and goods and distribute the proceeds to all, as any had need" (Acts 2:44). To live by dependence on communal monies and other necessities required them to trust that all would be fair and people would abide by their common agreement. It also required them to trust that their needs would be met by God. And it is clear that their attitude was effective and infectious for, as Luke says, many new disciples were added to the group.

In a similar way, Saint Peter told the Christian community that they must trust even when trials come. He wrote, "In this you rejoice, even if now for a little while you have had to suffer various trials, so that the genuineness of your faith — being more precious than gold that, though perishable, is tested by fire — may be found to result in praise and glory and honor when Jesus Christ is revealed" (1 Peter 1:6-7). We must have trust to endure the process, confident that we will come out stronger and closer to God by enduring the trials that come our way. Too often we run away from such trials, but the most important lessons and greatest teachings of life are generated through failure and suffering. If we do not have sufficient trust, however, we will never enter into the trial.

The classic example of Thomas' inability to trust his fellow apostles illustrates this point quite well. His trust and faith were weak and, therefore, he could only believe what he saw. When Jesus again appeared one week later, Thomas was forced to shamefacedly admit his lack of trust. His famous plea, "My Lord and my God," (John 20:28) demonstrates clearly that Thomas realized his error. Similarly, we must admit our own failures with respect to trust and then, do something about it.

Too often today people place trust in people and things that are either misguided or not worthy of our trust. We trust too completely in individuals, thinking that they are the solution to any and all of our problems. We trust too fully in institutions, ideologies, and material possessions that seem to satisfy our need and longing at the time. However, most all of us have sufficient experience to realize the hollowness present in the things of the world compared with the things of God. Imagine if we had sufficient trust in one another to live like those first disciples of Jesus described in the Acts of the Apostles. Imagine if we had sufficient trust to willingly engage trials and suffering, believing that such acts will actually be beneficial to us in the end. Imagine if we had sufficient trust to truly believe that God will never abandon us, but rather always walks by our side and, as the famous *Footprints* poem says, carries us when we need him most.

Let us renew our commitment to trust God. While the things of the world and their immediacy have a strong attraction for all, we learn from life experience that such ideas and material things are often hollow and without merit. Rather, let us do as the author of the book of Proverbs (3: 5) suggests, "Trust in the Lord with all your heart, and do not rely on your own insight."

Questions To Ponder:

1. What prevents me from placing complete trust in God? Why do I hold back?

2. When challenges arise, where do I place my trust? What more is necessary for me to completely trust that all will be provided for any situation?

3. What fears paralyze me, not allowing my full growth and potential in the sight of God?

4. What must I do to keep my priorities straight? Why do I at times place more trust in the things of the world then in God?

5. What aspect of my life needs to be reformed so that I can more faithfully follow where the Lord leads me?

"[Jesus said], "Do not fear, only believe" (Mark 5:36b).

Prayer: Lord, transform my head and heart to place my trust totally in you.

Trust As A Manifestation Of Faith

Theme: At times trust can be an elusive virtue in our contemporary society. Disappointment with the failures of others and even our possible belief that God cannot be trusted clouds our vision. We must, therefore, seek to reaffirm our trust in others and be trustworthy. Ultimately, we can and must place our total trust in God who is ever faithful and trustworthy.

Scripture To Ponder: Proverbs 3:5; 1 Timothy 6:11-19; John 20:19-29

If you have never witnessed or experienced a "trust walk" you are indeed in for a treat when the opportunity comes your way. Often utilized on youth retreats, the "trust walk" refers to one person leading a second individual, who is blindfolded, along some path that is strewn with obstacles, detours, and many twists and turns. This exercise requires skill on part of the leader to guide properly his partner to successfully and safely negotiate the various obstacles. However, probably the more difficult task is that of the one being led, for it necessitates that the person place his/her total trust in the guide. One must relinquish complete control and allow another to take the lead. The level of trust is indeed great, requiring one to surrender to the will of another, an activity which humans have never enjoyed.

While it might not be natural, trust as a manifestation of faith is a common theme in the Hebrew Bible. Abram placed his total trust in God when the Lord asked him to leave Ur, the land of his birth and travel to a new location with the promise that he would be the father of a great nation (Genesis 12:1-9). What a great Kierkegaardian "leap of faith" was necessary for Abram to listen to a strange God and believe that as a childless old man he would one day be the father of a great nation. Yet, somehow he managed to trust God (Genesis 15:1-21). His confidence was rewarded when Isaac was born (Genesis 21:1-7). Later when Abram, now with the expanded name of Abraham, was asked by God to sacrifice his son, his one chance for progeny, he again unhesitatingly made ready to do precisely what God commanded. It could not have made any sense to him, but somehow he held sufficient trust in God to be able to follow the Lord's plan (Genesis 22:1-19). Again, his trust was rewarded.

The long sojourn of the Israelites in the desert is another example of faith manifested through trust. The Israelites had no idea how to achieve their goal of arriving at the promised land and, therefore, God provided a cloud by day and fire by night to guide them (Exodus 13:21). Due to their disobedience it took forty years for the Israelites to return home, but in the end their trust brought them home. In the second or third (chapters 36-55) of his book of prophecy, Isaiah wrote to the Hebrews in exile in Babylon asking them to trust that God is benevolent and would rescue them from their bondage. Similarly, Ezekiel, writing to the same group of Hebrew exiles, analogized their community to dry bones strewn in the desert that God would gather and to which he would give life again (Ezekiel 37:1-14). The many examples of trust in God are appropriately and succinctly summarized in the book of Proverbs (3:5): "Trust in the Lord with all your heart, and do not rely on your own insight."

The New Testament is equally illustrative of how many men and women of faith manifested this great virtue through trust. When Jesus called the initial four apostles, Peter, his brother Andrew, James, and his brother John, most probably unlearned fishermen, they immediately left their livelihood and families and became his followers (Matthew 4:18-22). Clearly Jesus' call was inviting and powerful, but nonetheless the trust level manifested in the apostles' response was rather remarkable. Similarly lepers (Luke 17:11-19), the woman with the hemorrhage and Jairus (Mark 5:21-43), Bartimaeus (Mark 10:46-52), and even Nicodemus (John 3:1-21), a member of the Jewish Sanhedrin, manifested their faith by trusting that Christ could aid them, whether a physical cure for themselves or others or the needed instruction to understand the meaning of Jesus' message.

Jesus asked Martha to trust that Lazarus her brother would one day rise stating, "I am the resurrection and the life. Those who believe in me, even though they die, will live and everyone who lives and believes in me will never die" (John 11:25-26). As the author of the book of Proverbs summarized the need for trust, so too Jesus challenged the people of his day: "Do not fear, only believe" (Mark 5:36).

Manifesting faith through trust has never been easy, but it seems to be growing more difficult with time. Because we can basically control our person, we generally trust ourselves. Often this leads us through action to express: "If you want to get the job done, do it yourself." We shy away from placing our trust in others because we have no control, even when we might know the person well. Trust becomes even more difficult when past experience "teaches us" that a person is not as reliable as needed in a particular situation.

This inability to trust even extends to God. How often have we heard someone say or even spoken ourselves," God must not be listening or does not care since he does not answer my prayers." God certainly does listen and responds. Jesus says in the Sermon on the Mount (Matthew 7:7), "Ask and it will be given you; search, and you will find; knock, and the door will be opened to you." God's word is a guarantee of his response, but we might not be able to recognize or accept the Lord's plan in our life. Thus, we give up on God and in the process lose the opportunity of a lifetime.

Trust is something that does not arrive in a mature form, but rather grows with time, especially when speaking of people. We come to trust others based on our experience of them; we can physically see and experience how others respond. With God, however, things are different as we have no physical manifestations of God, save the Holy Spirit who is found in every person. But we can and must trust God to know what is best for us.

Trust must be a manifestation of our faith; it must become central to who we are and what we do. If we can trust ourselves, most assuredly we can trust God for the Lord knows us inside out. God trusts us; he gave us free will and allows us to operate without encumbrances. We do not live in a straitjacket; we have no constraints. Let us return the trust that God gives us, trust in the Father who created us, the Son who redeemed us, and the Holy Spirit, who sanctifies us and walks with us each step of our lives.

Questions To Ponder:

1. Who or what receives my trust? Can I trust God unreservedly?

2. Why do I at times place more trust in the world and its allurements than God?

3. What obstacles stand in my path that prevent me from believing that God can and must be trusted at all times and in all circumstances?

4. How have I at times been untrustworthy in my life? What can I do to make amends for these failures?

5. What must I do to establish greater trust between myself and family, co-workers, and neighbors?

"Those who trust in him will understand truth" (Wisdom 3:9a).

Prayer: Lord Jesus, help me to trust completely in you and, thereby, rest in the shadow of your wing.

Persistence Rewarded

Theme: "When the going gets tough, the tough get going." This expression should be a mantra for the Christian, but, unfortunately, at times we surrender, give up too readily and easily. We must realize, however, that persistence is necessary in all endeavors, including our relationship with God.

Scripture To Ponder: Genesis 18:20-32; Colossians 2:12-14; Luke 11:1-13

History records the expression, *Athanasius contra mundum*, which translates to Athanasius against the world. These words aptly express the situation in the fourth-century church when heresy almost reigned supreme, save Athanasius, a bishop who was a persistent and staunch defender of the faith. Athanasius was born into a Christian family in Alexandria, Egypt, in 295 CE. In his early twenties he was ordained and entered the service of Alexander, Bishop of Alexandria, whom he accompanied to the first ecumenical Council of the church at Nicaea in 325 CE when, among other matters, the heresy of Arianism, which claimed Jesus was not divine, was first condemned.

In 326, Alexander died and two years later Athanasius was selected to be the new Bishop of Alexandria. It was at this time that his career as a persistent defender of the faith began. His first opponent was Melitius, a fellow bishop, who believed that it was wrong to welcome back those who had turned their backs on the church. Athanasius triumphed in the struggle through a righteous and dogmatic campaign. His greatest nemesis, however, was the Arian heresy, which although condemned continued to grow and attract many to its theological perspective. In fact, the number of Arians was so great that Saint Jerome, the original translator of the scriptures into Latin (the Vulgate), once famously wrote, "The world awoke and found itself Arian."

Between 335 and 366 Athanasius, one of the few bishops in the Eastern Church who held the orthodox faith, was exiled on five different occasions for a total of seventeen years. Trumped-up charges, false testimony, and the events of the day combined to work against him, but each time Athanasius returned from exile he was more determined to defend the true faith. During his exiles, he wrote many important treatises, including *The Life of Antony*, a biography of Antony of the Desert, one of the first desert monks and a precursor to the monastic life.

Through tenacity and perseverance, Athanasius was able to prevail. He died in 373, living his last seven years in relative peace. His greatest triumph unfortunately came after his death at the Council of Constantinople in 381 when the Nicene-Constantinopolitan Creed, which contains the tenets of the faith that Athanasius so staunchly defended, was written and accepted. It was a testimony to Athanasius' persistence and dedication that the church triumphed over opposition.

Saint Athanasius' life stands as an example of the scriptural exhortation to be persistent in what we do in order to one day receive the reward of salvation. One might think on hearing the story of Abraham's conversation with God over the fate of Sodom and Gomorrah (Genesis 18:16-33) that the patriarch was quite bold. We recall how Abraham challenged God to stay his hand in the destruction of Sodom and Gomorrah, lest even ten innocent people should die. Abraham trusted God; he was persistent and challenged God's mercy and compassion, for he did not want any who were righteous to die with those who committed evil. Thus, through his persistence, Abraham was able to convince God that the city should not be destroyed even if there were only ten righteous people present there.

Jesus also called for persistence. In Luke 11:5-8 we hear the story of the one who comes to his neighbor at night. The favor requested was provided, not because of friendship, but as a result of the persistence of the one who was asking. Jesus, however, went further and said that our perseverance must be in our requests of God as well: "Ask and it will be given you; search, and you will find; knock and the door will be opened for you" (Luke 11:9). Jesus will answer our prayers. The response might not come when we expect or be of the nature we desire, but God will always meet our needs. We must remember, however, that too often our needs and our wants are not the same.

We need to be persistent. Life, as we know, is filled with obstacles, some detours, and even a few roadblocks. When these difficulties present themselves, we have two basic options. We can "throw in the towel," surrender, and say "we are defeated," or we can pick ourselves up, brush off the dust and dirt, and continue along the road, finding a new route if necessary to get where we need and want to be.

Persistence in our life, a form of trust in God, will eventually lead us home to the Lord. We must be persistent in our daily work. Sometimes the poor work ethic and pettiness of others gets us down, but this is when we must be persistent to do what is right simply because it is the right thing to do. We must work diligently at our tasks, giving them our best effort. We must also be persistent in relationships. Marriage requires daily vigilance; it is a daily task for two to act as one. All relationships, however, require our perseverance. Sometimes our persistence means challenging people — family members, friends, and colleagues — to move beyond where they presently find themselves to a new and higher plane. Sometimes persistence means demonstrating greater love and compassion toward others. Still, other times persistence in relationships means providing a listening ear and being present to one who needs us. We must be persistent with God and God's people and we must never give up on another, for God never gives up on any of us. Athanasius was a persistent and staunch defender of the faith. Lies, deceit, even exile could not deter him from his path. Certainly he was knocked off stride on several occasions, but through his persistence and trust in God, he always returned to continue the path that leads to God. We must, like Athanasius, doggedly pursue our goals, at work, in relationships, and especially with the Lord. Let us, therefore, be persistent in all that we do. Our reward in heaven will be great!

Questions To Ponder:

1. Why am I easily thrown off course from my objectives by hurdles or obstacles? Why am I at times insufficiently persistent to stay the course?

2. Why do I so easily give up on projects, people or difficult situations? Where is my faith in these events?

3. What lessons have I learned in life by failing in the past to be persistent in my various endeavors?

4. How can I manifest the expression, "When the going gets tough, the tough get going?"

5. What can I do to help those that I know to be more persistent in the various endeavors of their lives?

"I tell you, even though he will not get up and give him anything because he is his friend, at least because of his persistence he will get up and give him whatever he needs" (Luke 11:8).

Prayer: Lord, grant me the grace to never give up on myself, others, or you.

Perseverance Wins The Day

Theme: Life throws us many "curveballs," but we must, using a baseball image, hang in and continue to swing the bat. If we bailout not only will we miss the ball, but more importantly lose out on many opportunities, despite their difficulty, that will allow us to grow. Our task is to persevere and never give up.

Scripture to Ponder: Exodus 17:1-8; 2 Corinthians 11:21b-29; John 21:15-19

Like a shroud of darkness produced by the night, so a veil of silence enveloped him totally. What could be a worse fate for a composer of music? He was deaf and many times frustrated, but God, nevertheless, would not leave Ludwig van Beethoven alone. God pushed, sometimes gently and other times more forcefully, this often-reluctant composer, to reduce his greatest work through perseverance despite many significant obstacles.

The composition of Beethoven's *Missa Solemnis*, a lesser-known but highly significant work, would prove to be the composer's testament to faith and perseverance. In 1818, it was announced that Beethoven's longtime friend and supporter Archduke Rudolf of Austria was to be raised to the episcopacy. Beethoven wanted to write a great mass to celebrate the event. Most people who have studied Beethoven's life, including his most famous biographer, Alexander Thayer, have concluded that the great master was totally deaf by that time in his life. Can one imagine trying to compose great music yet not be able to hear the notes played, save as a memory in the brain?

The composition of the *Missa Solemnis* took five years. Several things made matters difficult for Beethoven. Two previous failures in composing church music had made him wary of a third attempt. He had family difficulties as well, especially a nasty custody battle over his nephew Karl. Additionally, Beethoven was writing his famous Ninth or Chorale Symphony simultaneously. Beethoven never gave up, however; he was a driven man.

Finally in May 1824, two sections of the mass along with the Ninth Symphony were premiered in a grand concert in Vienna. The Symphony was a rousing success, although the deaf Beethoven hardly realized the applause of the audience. The mass was received with less enthusiasm. Fortunately, through a patron the entire Mass was performed by itself one week later and received great acclaim. Over the years the *Missa Solemnis* has become a standard in the musical repertoire. Some musicologists call it Beethoven's *magnum opus*, not only because of its greatness in composition, but also as a testimony to the composer beating the odds.

The trust and perseverance demonstrated by Beethoven's ability to triumph over obstacles is illustrated in scripture. Moses could be called a reluctant deliverer. I am sure he would have been more than happy, after his escape from Egypt, to live the life of a shepherd, raise a family, and be an ordinary person. But God appeared to him and issued a challenge which he could not reject. Moses was also asked to trust God and persevere through a long forty-year trek through the desert, a journey elongated by the infidelity of the Jews. Yet, while his people went wayward on numerous occasions, he never abandoned his trust in Yahweh. His trust and perseverance eventually brought the community of Israel to the promised land.

In the New Testament, Saint Paul wrote to his friend Timothy (2 Timothy 4:2) and told him, "Proclaim the message; be persistent whether the time is favorable or unfavorable; convince, rebuke, and encourage, with the utmost patience in teaching." We encounter many teachers along the road of life-parents, relatives, mentors, educators, coaches, and others who have been given a special ministry to teach. They are to teach whether it is convenient or inconvenient; they are never to lose heart. It is a difficult task to which all who bear the name of Christian are called. It is the perseverance that teachers show that will one day be manifested in the words and actions of those to whom they minister.

Let us also remember, however, that we do not take up this difficult task alone. In baptism, we become children of God and members of the Christian community which calls each individual to help the whole group find the sometimes unseen God and answer the challenges which come our way. When we work together we can better negotiate the hurdles and obstacles, make straight the crooked paths, and better traverse the road of life.

We need to be persistent in our lives. Beethoven had an inner drive, the voice of God, which pushed him to produce a master work as a testimony of faith. Through perseverance the task was completed and we are the benefactors of that persistence. We need to be persistent, whether it is convenient or inconvenient, in prayer, as teachers of the faith, and as models of Christian love to the world. Let us accept and persevere through the challenges of life so as to make the sometimes unseen God more visible today and each day of our lives.

Questions To Ponder:

1. How much am I willing to pay to accomplish a task — to what lengths will I go?

2. When was the last time I felt inadequate to the situation, unable to answer the call before me? How did I react?

3. What has been the greatest challenge of the past that has prevented me from persevering and led me to give up?

4. What did I learn from my past failures to persevere through the challenges of life? How did I grow from these events?

5. What have I learned about myself when I had the opportunity and found the courage to persevere through some difficult situation?

"Ask, and it will be given to you; search, and you will find; knock, and the door will be opened for you" (Matthew 7:7).

Prayer: Lord Jesus, never allow me to never give up in my pursuit of you.

Strength Through Weakness

Theme: Life throws many challenges our way and we at times "throw up our hands" and say that is all too much. However, at these low points, when we feel weak and vulnerable, we have the opportunity to realize that our current weakness can in reality become a strength that will lead us to victory and eventually to eternal life. Let us transform our weaknesses into strengths this day.

Scripture To Ponder: Ezekiel 2:2-5; 2 Corinthians 12:7-10; Mark 6:1-6

Kara, a lonely falcon who lived in the forest, was different from all other birds of prey. After spending a good deal of time as a hunter, Kara had vowed that she would never again harm a living animal. The other animals of the forest were instinctively afraid of Kara, whose native power and ferocity drove others away. She wanted to be accepted by other animals and thus had to find a way to show another side of her character.

One day, while flying high above the forest, she spied a mother dove returning to her nest in the crevice of the mountain cliff. A hawk had also seen the dove and turned toward her, flying as fast as possible, aiming for a kill and a meal. Kara, however, outraced the hawk and beat him off before he could inflict harm on the mother dove. The dove, a bit shaken by the incident, was able to return home, although she was quite confused and unsure of the strange behavior of this falcon. Word got around the forest of what Kara had done; the other animals slowly began to change their attitudes toward her.

During the summer months, Kara ate the produce of the land since she had vowed never to kill again. Initially this new food was not very appetizing, but over time she began to enjoy the berries, seeds, and various fruits provided by the forest. The animals in the area, the rabbits, squirrels, and other birds, began to trust Kara; the natural enemies began to accept one another for who they were, not what they would do or what they could provide. They began to find strength in one another.

In the winter months food was less plentiful for Kara, for unlike the other animals of the forest who instinctively gathered food for safe storage during the fall months, Kara had no reserve and was at times unable to find her daily sustenance. Her neighbors in the forest noticed the plight of their new friend and decided to share with her. Each day Kara would soar high into the sky, as falcons do, and return later to her home in the crevice of the cliff. She and her friends ate dinner together, each animal supplying something from their winter cache. Kara also brought a special food, one never seen in the forest, which grew from the rocks near her home.

One day, as was typical, Kara flew high into the sky above the forest, but that evening her friends were disappointed as she did not return. Where had she gone? No one was sure. However, when the animals of the forest came to Kara's perch they noticed that the special food which she had brought to their daily meals was still growing from the crevice in the rock. Kara was gone but her presence would live forever.

Joseph Girzone's Christological tale, *Kara the Lonely Falcon*, gives us much food for thought in speaking of the strength we possess by our ability to accept our weakness. Others, in turn are then able to accept us for who we are. Scripture provides a similar message of the need to find strength through weakness.

The prophet Ezekiel had to work against significant odds when God sent him to the obstinate and rebellious Hebrew people in exile in Babylon. Ezekiel realizes that he and his message will not be accepted for what they are; the people are blind to their need for God. Despite his reception, Ezekiel carries out God's plan by prophesying in order to show the people that a prophet has been in their midst (Ezekiel 2:5).

In Mark's gospel (6:1-6), Jesus shows great disappointment in the people of his hometown who have no faith and, therefore, cannot accept the Lord for who he was. The people say, "Where did he get all this? What is this wisdom that has been given to him? What deeds of power are being done by his hands! Is not this the carpenter, the son of Mary and the brother of James and Joses and Judas and Simon, and are not his sisters here with us?" (Mark 6:2-3). The people express no weakness, no hunger or need for God. The inability of the people to accept Ezekiel or Jesus, or to demonstrate their need for the Lord, kept God at arm's length. The opportunity to encounter God was missed.

Saint Paul, on the other hand, realized the need for God in his life. Unlike the Hebrews of Ezekiel's day or the Jews of Jesus' time, Paul was able to acknowledge his need for God. Paul was humbled and accepted his weakness: "So I will boast all the more gladly of my weaknesses, so that the power of Christ may dwell in me. Therefore, I am content with weaknesses, insults, hardships, persecutions and calamities for the sake of Christ; for whenever I am weak, then I am strong" (2 Corinthians 12:9b-10).

All people seek acceptance and strength in their lives, but the great tendency is to submit to the pressure of discovering acceptance in the manner and style of the day. Adults seek acceptance in business as professionals through the language we use, the clothes we wear, and the priorities of our actions. Young people seek acceptance and strength as part of the group, even if compromise is necessary to join.

It is difficult these days to place our trust in the Lord and through that faith, to be accepted for who we are. We want to be more like others and we refuse to admit our inabilities and weaknesses. Yet, it is through weakness that the strength we need can be found. Kara the falcon found there was no need to be powerful; she could be weak and gain acceptance. The other animals of the forest not only accepted her, they shared their lives with her. Jesus willingly chose to be weak by taking on human form to provide the ultimate example and eventually ransom us from death and lead us to eternal life (Philippians 2:6-11). In a society oriented toward seeking merit and manifesting demonstrations of power, it is difficult to accept weakness and see it as a vehicle to strength. Yet, by turning our lives over to the

Lord in faith, we will find the strength that only God can give. Let us, therefore, seek acceptance for who we are, acknowledge our weaknesses, and through this search find strength for God's work, today and each day of our lives.

Questions To Ponder:

1. Why am I ashamed of my weaknesses? How can I utilize them effectively to grow stronger in other areas?

2. What can I do if my weaknesses paralyze me, not allowing me to move forward and meet my responsibilities and accomplish my goals?

3. What is my greatest weakness? What can I do to utilize it in a positive way, finding strength through weakness?

4. How have I negotiated through the situations in life where I felt too weak to accomplish the task?

5. How have I been able to aid others to transform their weaknesses into strengths, defeats into victories?

"Blessed are the meek, for they will inherit the earth" (Matthew 5:5).

Prayer: Lord, allow me to accept my weakness and thereby gain the strength that only you can provide.

Bearing The Cross With Jesus

Theme: Life inevitably brings many challenges that need to be negotiated. These metaphorical crosses need to be born with great dignity and perseverance. We can learn a lot from enduring the pain and suffering of the cross and thus we should never run from them. Rather, let us bear the cross as did Jesus and in the end find eternal life.

Scripture To Ponder: 1 Samuel 8:4-22; 2 Timothy 4:1-8; Luke 9: 23-27

The greatest paradox of Christianity was best expressed by Jesus himself: "For those who want to save their life will lose it, and those who lose their life for my sake will find it" (Matthew 16:25). Like all paradoxes, Jesus' words on first examination seem unbelievable, but closer scrutiny and prayerful reflection show us that not only are the words true, but they ultimately lead his followers to the cross, a reality which Saint Paul declared as, "foolishness to those who are perishing, but to us who are being saved, it is the power of God" (1 Corinthians 1:18). The cross continues to mystify Christians 2000 years later, for as strange as it may seem, it is only by bearing the cross with Jesus, with its pain and daily dying, that we find life.

In June, 1958, Bishop Fulton Sheen, then at the height of his popularity and fame through his television ministry, public speaking, and numerous books and essays, gave a commencement address which spoke of our need to embrace Jesus' cross. In his speech the bishop described the heightened state of the cold war, existent since the end of World War II, between the Soviet Union and the United States. Sheen characterized the Soviet Union as a nation under the weight of the cross, but with no Christ to bear it. He referred to the severe plight of Soviet society that continued thirteen years after the end of the war.

During the war 30 million people died, almost half were Russians. Besides the great carnage of death and injury wrought on the Soviet people, scars were still present in economic hardship, lack of food, clothing, and shelter, and a totalitarian government that opted entirely for the communist elite. The Soviet Union was a nation that bore a great cross, but it was done without the aid of Christ, who was a non-entity in the ideology of atheism that the communist government promoted.

The 1950s in the United States saw a much different picture. Bishop Sheen characterized our nation as a country with Christ but no cross. America, which suffered the least damage to its people and way of life of any of the major belligerents, emerged from the war as leader of the free world. Economically the country saw a boom period; the American people clearly saw themselves atop the pack in the race for productivity and a higher standard of living. The boon in the economy was also experienced in organized religion, especially Christianity, which experienced a renewed enthusiasm. The United States had Christ, as evidenced by religious practice, but it had no cross.

Bishop Sheen's comparison was used to show, as the words of Jesus indicate, that there is a need for the world to have both the cross and Christ; one without the other results in the state of incompleteness that must be satisfied. The life of Jesus and the message of scripture tell us that the cross will be part of our lives and that we must embrace it, rather than run away or reject it, in order to find eternal life. We are called to trust that God knows what he is doing. It seems this is all wrong, backwards, and foolish. But the reality is, as Jesus reminds us, "Unless a grain of wheat falls into the earth and dies, it remains just a grain of wheat; but if it dies, it bears much fruit" (John 12:24).

The primary example of one who embraced the cross was Jesus himself. Saint John's narrative portrays Jesus' greatest victory, his highest exultation, in his crucifixion and painful death. On Good Friday, Jesus was not dragged to the cross kicking and screaming. Rather, he went voluntarily; he chose to die that we could have eternal life. If Jesus had not embraced the cross our faith would be meaningless.

Jesus knew his future fate and professed it openly. The gospels tell us that on three different occasions, Christ predicted his ignominious death, yet he continued the journey toward his final fate in Jerusalem. Jesus knew, as the author of Ecclesiastes (3:1-2) told us, "For everything there is a season, and a time for every matter under heaven; a time to be born, and a time to die." His death brought life for us, but this great paradox of our faith was not possible without his embrace of the cross.

The apostles, especially Peter, were not ready for Jesus' cross and they ran from it with all due speed and strength. Immediately after the Lord declared Peter to be "rock," the one upon whom the church would be built, the apostle ran from the cross: "God forbid it, Lord! This must never happen to you." Jesus' response to Peter's rejection of the cross is swift and severe: "Get behind me, Satan! You are a stumbling block to me; for you are setting your mind not on divine things but on human things" (Matthew 16:22-23).

Jesus provided a general teaching for all his followers: "If any want to become my followers, let them deny themselves and take up their cross and follow me. For those who want to save their life will lose it, and those who lose their life for my sake will find it" (Matthew 16:22-25). Eventually Peter came to understand the need for the cross in human life: "In this you rejoice, even if now for a little while you have had to suffer various trials, so that the genuineness of your faith — being more precious than gold that, though perishable, is tested by fire — may be found to result in praise and glory and honor when Jesus Christ is revealed" 1 Peter 1:6-7).

Mary, the mother of God, was another one who lived her life by embracing the cross. When Jesus was presented in the temple, Simeon told Mary, "This child is destined for the falling and the rising of many in Israel, and to be a sign that will be opposed, so that the inner thoughts of many will be revealed — and a sword will pierce your own soul too" (Luke 2:34b-35). Some years later, Mary was again forced to endure the cross when Jesus was "lost" for three days in Jerusalem, only to be found in the temple speaking with the Jewish teachers who ministered there (Luke 2:41-51). Although scripture does not recount the great middle period of Jesus' life in Nazareth with his parents, it is certain that Mary endured, as do all parents, several other trials with her son. Tradition says that Mary met Jesus on the *via dolorosa*; she was beneath the cross when her son, Jesus, was crucified (John 19:25).

The examples of Jesus and Mary have been followed by many Christians throughout the centuries. The great saints and martyrs embraced the crosses in their lives and used them to triumph over the forces that threatened them in their task of being disciples of Jesus. The litany of saints and martyrs of Christian history, those who embrace the cross and used it to bring others closer to Christ, continues today with such names as Dietrich Bonhoeffer and Oscar Romero.

Christianity is not an easy way of life. The great task of Christians today is to see how victory can be snatched from defeat, how good can come from bad, how wrong can be converted to right. To do nothing, to say, "It is too difficult" or "I cannot be involved — it is too messy," or "I do not have the time," is to run from the cross which we must embrace. The crosses of life will come our way. If we run from them then the challenge is not met and we cannot grow, but if we pick up and carry the cross, if we walk the road that Jesus walked, then we will not only grow, we will be found worthy of God and eternal life. The author of the book of Wisdom (3:4-6) placed the cross in perspective: "For though in the sight of others they have been punished, their hope is full of immortality. Having been disciplined a little, they will receive great good, because God tested them and found them worthy of himself; like gold in the furnace he tried them and like a sacrificial burnt offering he accepted them."

Christianity is a paradox. It does not make sense that we must die in order to find life, yet our faith teaches us the truth of this statement. One cannot escape the cross, but if we accept it as did

Christ, if we combine the cross with the presence of Jesus, then the difficulties and pain we suffer become the means to salvation. We certainly do not look for the cross, but it will find us whether we like it or not. Let us, therefore, embrace the cross and know that its weight when born alongside Jesus will bring us home. May the Good Friday experience be lived each day as we journey toward the kingdom of God, present today, and in eternal life.

Questions To Ponder:

1. How can I better carry my cross and assist others with the ones they carry?

2. Why do I run from the various crosses, the challenges of my life?

3. What were some of the great lessons of life that I learned when forced to endure a cross?

4. How can I better live the paradox of Christianity, by dying to self so as to live better today for others?

5. Who are the people in my life who have born crosses? What can I do to emulate their fidelity?

"And being found in human form, he humbled himself and became obedient to the point of death—even death on a cross" (Philippians 2:8).

Prayer: Father, help me to carry the cross as bravely as Jesus.

Reliance Upon God

Theme: Placing our trust in God and relying on others to meet their responsibilities does, at times, require a leap of faith. Yet, we cannot simply live life as solo operators, but rather must work with others and trust in God's abiding presence. To do anything else is inconsistent with our Christian call.

Scripture To Ponder: Genesis 22:1-18; Romans 8:31-34; Mark 9:2-10

Sophocles, the famous Greek dramatist, graced the world with his many plays. His famous trilogy of *Oedipus Rex*, *Oedipus at Colonnus*, and *Antigone* is his greatest legacy. In *Oedipus Rex* there is a famous section known as the *Riddle of the Sphinx*. In order for Oedipus to gain entry to his desired destination he must solve this famous riddle: What has four legs in the morning, two legs in the afternoon, and three legs in the evening? The answer is a human being. In the morning, the first period of our life, we crawl; we need all fours, legs and arms, to move and get around. In the great middle or afternoon of our life we walk upright on two legs. In the twilight of our life we often need some assistance, such as a cane or a helping hand; we use three legs in this stage of our life.

The riddle of the sphinx tells us something powerful about our reliance on others. When we are infants we need the support of others. We are totally dependent as young children on others, for food, clothing, shelter, love, in short all our needs. As children, we trust that all will be provided. We don't worry; our trust is absolute in those who care for us. When we are old enough to walk, we begin to rely on ourselves. We venture out, just a little at first, but later with ever more bold steps. We try things for ourselves. As time goes on, our ability to trust in others begins to wane. Life throws us curves; we get knocked down and kicked around.

Our trust shifts to a more exclusive reliance on the tangible and visible things of our world. We begin to say that we need to do it ourselves; we cannot rely on others any longer. Others just might not come through for us! When we get older, when we need that third leg, we again begin to trust in others. We can no longer do everything that we once could do. We need the aid of other people, for the complex and sometimes even the simple everyday tasks of life.

Scripture, like the riddle of the sphinx, tells us something about relying on others, specifically our need to trust God. The Genesis account of Abraham's test of faith with his son Isaac illustrates this point. Abraham was an adult; he could walk properly and speak for himself. Yet Abraham placed his total reliance, his total life, in God's hands; he had complete faith. We recall how God told Abraham that he would be the father of a great nation. Isaac was Abraham and Sarah's only child, the fruit of their old age. God then asked Abraham to sacrifice his one chance for heritage. For three days, Abraham and his son Isaac journeyed, yet Abraham's faith never wavered; his trust in God was absolute. He was always ready to do what God asks. In the end, he received his reward as the father of a great nation. Still today Jews see Abraham as their father in faith.

In 2 Timothy 1:8-10, we hear about the obedience of Jesus to God the Father. Jesus was human, like you and me, yet his faith, unlike ours, never vacillated. Jesus was obedient to God to the point of death on the cross. Because of his obedience, Jesus was exalted and has become for us the great intercessor to God. This is why many prayers in the Christian tradition invoke Christ as the one through whom we make our intercession. Jesus' reliance on God was complete and total.

Conversion is necessary if we are to trust completely in the Lord. In the story of the Transfiguration (Matthew 17:1-9, Mark 9:2-8, Luke 9:28-36) Jesus is changed in appearance, but this transformation is temporary. The more important conversion is found with the apostles. Peter, James, and John were always there, it seemed, when important events happened in the life of the Jesus. These men were the ones who were converted on the inside, where it counted and was permanent. Their conversion was to a life of total reliance on God. Certainly the apostles failed; they had their problems. But their faith in and obedience to Jesus was now a part of their being; they were changed forever.

If we were asked upon whom or what do we rely, what would be our honest answer? Some would answer that they rely on the material things of this life. These things are tangible, useable, and reliable, at least so it seems; we know for certain they exist. Some people rely on others in their life, family, friends or associates. Some rely totally on themselves.

All of us to a lesser or greater extent need to be converted to a complete and unqualified reliance on God. Abraham relied on God and became the father of a great nation. Jesus relied on the Father and was exalted to glory. If we rely on God and have complete faith, then we too will find the rewards of God.

Let us follow the example of Abraham and Jesus. Let us not be dominated by the world, as the riddle of the sphinx suggests. Let us hope and pray that if the world placed us on trial for our faith and reliance on God, there would be sufficient evidence to convict us!

Questions To Ponder:

1. When adversity strikes or challenges arise, to whom or what do I turn for strength and answers?

2. Why does my trust in God waiver?

3. What prevents me from having greater trust in those around me? Why do I always want to do it myself instead of asking for assistance?

4. What needs to be transformed in me so I can trust more fully and completely, in others and in God?

5. What is the level of my self-esteem? Do I trust myself sufficiently that God will give me the capability to complete the tasks and meet the responsibilities of my life?

"Trust in the Lord with all your heart, and do not rely on your own insight" (Proverbs 3:5).

Prayer: Lord Jesus, help me to always place my trust in you.

God Challenges Us

Theme: "No pain, no gain" is a common expression by athletes who realize that challenging themselves physically is necessary to attain their goals. Similarly, if we are to advance in our relationship with God, we need to accept the challenges, painful though they at times may be, to develop and be the people God called us to be. Challenge is good; let us accept the trial as we grow in holiness.

Scripture To Ponder: Wisdom 6:12-16;
1 Thessalonians 4:13-18; Matthew 25:1-13

Is the life you lead one for which you want to be remembered? That very challenging and thought-provoking question certainly must have come to the mind of the famous Swedish scientist Alfred Nobel when in the common everyday exercise of reading the morning paper he discovered the challenge to trust God before his very eyes.

Nobel was born in 1833 to a scientist and his wife. From his earliest days it was evident to everyone that Alfred was gifted intellectually. He read voraciously every book he could find, but he especially loved literary classics. By the time he was fifteen he could read, write, and speak four languages besides his native Swedish. Although he showed promise in the "humanities" area, it was his love of science and his desire to be an inventor, like his father, that most excited him.

When Nobel was sixteen, he had exhausted the educational possibilities of his native district in Sweden and thus decided to move away for more training. He first went to Paris and then across the Atlantic to the United States where he spent four years studying science and engineering principles, ideas that had become that much more important after the onset of the Industrial Revolution in the latter decades of the eighteenth century.

With his education complete, Nobel returned to his native

land and began to tinker around in his laboratory, creating an invention or two, but nothing of any significance. In the 1860s, however, he began to conduct experiments with nitroglycerin, a highly volatile and unstable substance. In one experiment there was an explosion and Alfred's younger brother was killed. The experience crushed Nobel in one way, but in another it became the catalyst to find a way to harness the energy of this substance and make it of practical use to the world.

Nobel discovered a functional use of nitroglycerin, but it came about quite accidentally. One day in his workshop, he noticed that some of the nitroglycerin, which is a liquid above 55 degrees Fahrenheit, had leeched into some packing material which surrounded the many bottles of chemicals sent him for his various experiments. Nobel found that this third substance, made from the initial two, had all the energy capacity and blasting potential of nitroglycerin, but it was stable and, thus, could be better controlled. Without knowing it, Alfred Nobel had invited dynamite.

The uses of dynamite throughout the world made Nobel a famous and very rich man overnight. Mountains could be blasted away to make room for railroads. However, his new invention could also be placed into bombs, projectiles, and other weapons of war. With patents received in 1867 and 1868, first in the United States and later in Great Britain, for dynamite and blasting caps, and with the discovery of oil on land he owned in the state of Russia, he became one of the richest men in the world as well as one of the most famous. He could sit back, relax, and enjoy life.

Alfred's serenity came to an abrupt halt one day when he picked up the morning paper and read the headline, "Dynamite King Dies." The story and obituary in the paper were erroneous; he was very much alive and well. Nobel decided to read the article, however, in order to know what people would think of him after his death. Besides all the normal facts and dates of an obituary, he read a description which labeled him as the "merchant of death." The expression disturbed the scientist greatly. Certainly the comment came in reference to his association with dynamite, but this did not lighten the blow. Nobel realized at that moment that the life he had led was not the life for which he wanted to be remembered. He was not ready to meet the Lord.

Something needed to be done to correct how people perceived him and to make him ready for his death. The past was history; its record was etched in stone. The future was something, however, over which Nobel had some control. Alfred was a rich man. How, he pondered, could that money be put to a positive use. He decided to change his will, leaving his vast fortune in trust to a committee which each year would select people who, in theory and practice, had made positive contributions to the furthering of humankind. Thus, in 1901, five years after his death, the first Nobel Prizes were awarded, initially in five areas, physics, chemistry, literature, medicine, and the famous Nobel Peace Prize. Later, in 1968 and thereafter, a prize in economics was added.

Is the life you lead one for which you want to be remembered? The same question that haunted Alfred Nobel must be asked of all of us. The challenge of God, to trust him completely, is presented to us in many ways every day, but do we have the eyes of faith to see it and the courage to act upon it?

Isaiah speaks of the challenge of God that comes at the beginning of our life of faith. The last third of Isaiah (chapters 56-66) is written after the Hebrews' return from the Babylonian exile. The words are, therefore, very futuristic and prophetic: "I am coming to gather all nations and tongues. ...From them I will send survivors to the nations, ...to the coast lands far away that have not heard of my fame or seen my glory; and they shall declare my glory among the nations." (Isaiah 66:18b, 19a, c) God will gather the nations, and through representatives, will send a challenge to all. Some will hear and heed the challenge, others will hear and reject the warning, and still others will not listen at all. This is the first, the initial challenge of trusting God.

How does God challenge us in the vast middle of our life, the day-to-day existence in which we all live? Certainly the challenge of God is present in many ways, but maybe especially when things are not going the way we envisioned them to proceed. In the Letter to the Hebrews, we read, "My child, do not regard lightly the discipline of the Lord or lose heart when you were punished by him … Endure trials for the sake of discipline" (Hebrews 12:5b, 7a). The discipline of the Lord might be recast as a challenge to trust that comes from God when things do not work out as expected.

Think of the challenges that sometimes come into our lives. It is a challenge from God when we lose our job or we do not receive the promotion that we have earned or the raise that is justifiably ours. How do we react to such a challenge? When we become sick — especially if we are hospitalized or incapacitated so that we cannot continue our normal routine — this is a challenge to trust God as well. Is our reaction anger or do we try to find out how God speaks in such moments? Failure can also be a challenge from God. Whether we fail in a relationship, a business venture, or any personal trust, the presence of God is there. How do we respond? Most commonly, God challenges us when the prayers we honestly say do not receive the answer we expect or want. Do we accept God's answer or do we search other places for the answer we want? In general how do we react to the challenge of God in the difficulties of life?

How do we react to God's presence when things seem to be going fine? When we are sailing along with not a care in the world, do the presence of God and the challenge therein make an impression on us? It might be even more difficult to find God and accept the challenge when the sun shines in our life!

God's final challenge to trust comes at the end of our days in this world. We have received an initial challenge through the baptismal call to holiness, a message that goes out to the entire world. This challenge continues with God's "discipline" of humankind. What about the final challenge? In Luke's gospel (13:24-25), Jesus spoke about the elect and rejected at the end of time:

Strive to enter through the narrow door; for many, I tell you, will try to enter and not be able. When once the owner of the house has got up and shut the door, and you begin to stand outside and to knock at the door saying, "Lord, open to us," then in reply he will say to you," I do not know where you come from."

God will decide who has heeded the challenge, who has passed the test of trust. Those who have been found worthy, those who have answered the call, will be the elect who enter through the narrow gate. Those who have refused to answer the challenge of God will find themselves on the outside where "there will be we will be weeping and gnashing of teeth" (Luke 13:28a).

The presence of God is all around us, but can we see it, sense the challenge, and act accordingly? God is present in nature — the beauty of the sunrise and the sunset, the power of the surf pounding on a deserted beach, and the gentleness of a soft, cooling summer breeze. God is present in the events — the everyday events, the high points, the ecstasies, the triumphs, and the difficulties, the defeats, and the tragedies of this life. God is most especially present in people — family members, loved ones, business associates, and colleagues. And yes, God is even present in those we do not like or do not know. God is present in nature, events, and people but how do we react?

What is our response to the challenge of God in our lives? Alfred Nobel had lived the majority of his life as a rich, famous, and seemingly content man, but then an erroneous obituary made him realize that the life he had lived to that time was not one for which he wanted to be remembered. What will it take to shake us up sufficiently to face the challenge of God and trust him in our lives? Only you can answer!

Questions To Ponder:

1. What changes and developments in my life are required in order to find my true path to God and life eternal?

2. Why do I resist the call of the Lord, especially when I know that change is necessary in my life?

3. How has God recently challenged me to move in a different direction and answer his call to greater holiness?

4. How do I react when people challenge me? Am I defensive and refuse to listen or do I accept the critique and try to improve?

5. What amends have I made to others when I failed to meet my responsibilities to them?

"These are they who have come out of the great ordeal; they have washed their robes and made them white in the blood of the Lamb" (Revelation 7:14).

Prayer: Lord, may my actions always demonstrate pride in being your disciple."

Nothing Is Too Difficult For God

Theme: Living in a finite world challenges us to perceive the infinite possibilities of God. Because we have been disappointed in others or the perception that God is not listening, we at times place God and others in a "straitjacket;" we limit God. We must allow God to act, realizing that nothing is impossible for God.

Scripture To Ponder: 1 Samuel 17:1-54; Act 9:1-19; Luke 1:26-28

In mathematics the concept of "pi" is an example of a radical. It is a term which cannot be precisely or fully defined or known. We all learn in grade school that pi is 3.1416.... Pi cannot be fully known because it consists of an infinite string of numbers that come after the decimal point. Unlike the number 100 or even 50.50 which have definite and very precise values, pi is not totally definable.

Since pi is an infinite number, we can only approximate its value. Some people have memorized the number pi to 200 places or more. One could memorize pi to 200 times 200 places and still have only an infinitesimal understanding of the number for infinity is forever. We who live a finite existence can only understand something that has bounds. Thus, we make an approximation for pi and say it is good enough. We make a compromise; we cheat a bit. We use pi to calculate certain quantities that we need for building or designing some object. Our approximation is usually adequate for our needs.

Placing limits on things is the human reality. Humans can go only so far in understanding the infinite. We have never seen anything that is infinite and thus we can only guess at what infinity is. We know it is big, that is goes on forever. But this can lead to confusion, because we can only think on the finite level. When we place limits or boundaries on things it makes life more understandable, at least we can recognize that which we are trying to define.

God is infinite, that is what we have been taught since the time we first began to understand what others told us. The Hebrews believed that Yahweh was infinite, all powerful, all knowing, and omnipresent. Christians believe that Jesus is like the Father in all things and, therefore, is infinite. Jesus displayed compassion and love which were beyond human understanding.

Since God is infinite, how can we understand God? We make an attempt to understand God by placing limits on him. We set boundaries that God cannot exceed so as to make possible some understanding of the infinite. Theologically speaking, I suspect, there is a need to speak of God in some finite manner. Without some bounds, God is unapproachable on an intellectual level.

Our propensity to place limits on the infinite can lead to problems, however, when we speak of our faith and trust in God. Human beings for centuries have been placing restrictions, limits, and boundaries on their faith in God. The Hebrews were a people who constantly wanted a sign that God was with them in their struggles. They were never satisfied. God wrought the plagues in Egypt, parted the Red Sea, provided water and food in the desert, and made Israel victorious in battle when they conquered the promised land. Yet, the Hebrews continued to look for signs. The limits of their faith placed limits on their belief in God's providence. The stories of the judges and prophets of ancient Israel describe over and over again the people's inability to believe that God truly is infinite and will never abandon his greatest creation, the human race.

People in the time of Jesus also wanted signs. God was again placed in a straightjacket, tied up, and not allowed to be infinite. The limited faith shown by the Pharisees and other religious leaders of Jewish society was applied to their unbelief in Jesus. People were amazed each time Jesus performed something miraculous. It was only because people had little faith that the actions of an infinite God were so striking. As Jesus said to his followers, "If you had faith the size of a mustard seed, you could say to this mulberry tree, 'Be uprooted and planted in the sea' and it would obey you'" (Luke 17:6).

People today are still placing limits on God. It is only natural; it is the only way we can confidently know something of God. Yet, we transfer our limitations on the concept of God to our faith and trust in the Lord. We refuse to believe that God truly can do all things. We constantly need to be reminded of Jesus' words, "For God all things are possible" (Mark 10:27b).

To believe in the infinite is a great challenge. Christianity is such a belief. To speak of God as a person, to draw a picture of God or think of him standing before us is at best an approximation. It is the best we can do, however, and thus is important and useful. We cannot, however, hold such limitations on our faith and what God can do for us. God truly is infinite and thus capable of all things. When we speak with and listen to God in prayer, let us remember to keep the doors of possibility open. God knows our needs before we can even share them with him. Let us allow God's gift of faith to be boundless, infinite. If we can do this, then we can truly believe that nothing is impossible with God!

Questions To Ponder:

1. Why do I at times unconsciously limit God's ability to act in our world?

2. What limits have I placed on others? Why do I too often feel people will not meet their responsibilities?

3. What limits have I placed on myself; why do I think that I cannot achieve great things with the help of God?

4. When was the last time I gave up in a difficult situation? What did I learn from my failure to persevere?

5. What keeps me from believing that with God all things are truly possible?

"Seek the Lord while he may be found, call upon him while he is near" (Isaiah 55:6).

Prayer: Father, open my mind and heart fully to experience your presence in all things.

"Fear Is Useless —
What Is Needed Is Trust"

Theme: Sometimes we might think we are on "mission impossible," that there is no solution to the difficulties or challenges we face. While life at times can drag us down, scripture and history clearly provide evidence that if we persevere and demonstrate faith, that nothing is impossible for those who trust in God.

Scripture To Ponder: 1 Kings 19:9-13; Romans 9:1-5; Matthew 14:22-33

Great challenges and difficult situations often evoke the words, "It can't be done." History, however, is replete with examples of people, who with faith and trust, proved that problematic situations can be solved and difficult tasks can be accomplished. People said that it was impossible for humans to fly; it was a crazy idea. However, in December 1903 at Kitty Hawk, North Carolina, two brothers who worked as bicycle repairmen, Wilbur and Orville Wright, proved that it was possible. That first powered flight lasted less than one minute, but today millions of people each day board airplanes, fly hundreds of miles for work or recreation, and never give the experience a second thought.

It was thought that Mount Everest, the highest point of land on earth, could not be conquered. However, in May of 1953 Edmund Hilary, John Hunt, and their British expedition team reached the summit. After over sixty years, the mountain has been conquered so many times that the feat merits only a mention in the back page of the daily newspaper.

In the world of sport, it was thought humanly impossible for a person to run a mile in less than four minutes. Glenn Cunningham, the great middle distance runner from Kansas, had held the world mark of 4:06.7 for several years. However, on a cold and drizzly day in May 1954, Roger Bannister, a British medical student, made history when he crossed the finish line and broke the tape in 3:59.4. Today top-notch high school milers approach this magic barrier.

In the early part of this century the idea of space travel was a thing of comic books and the science fiction novels of H.G. Wells. In 1961, however, the United States took up the challenge and made a goal to reach the moon before the end of the decade. In an event witnessed by millions, Neil Armstrong, on July 20, 1969 set foot on the moon. His words still echo in our ears, "That's one small step for man, one giant leap for mankind."

Challenges cause us to question and possibly say, "It can't be done," but as history and the gospels suggest, for a person of faith, all things are possible. Saint Mark's account (5:21-43) of Jairus, "framed" about the story of the woman with a hemorrhage, is a powerful story of how faith can conquer fear. Jairus, we are told by the evangelist, was an official, who, most probably, was well known in the community, if not in the nation of Israel as a whole. Yet, his position did not shelter him from a great burden, a challenge which caused him great pain — his daughter was near death. Jairus had faith, however, and he knew that Jesus was in the area. He threw himself at the Lord's feet and asked him to help. "My little daughter is at the point of death. Come and lay your hands on her so that she may be made well, and live" (5:23). The people in Jairus' house, in contrast, did not believe; they had no faith. "Your daughter is dead," they said, "why trouble the teacher any further?" Jesus discounted the report using significant words: "Do not fear, only believe" (5:35b, 36b). The people laughed and ridiculed Jesus, but, as always in the end, the Lord is the victor; he is triumphant. Fear is conquered and doubt is dispelled. The little girl was restored to complete health and returned to her parents.

The woman with the hemorrhage presents a similar case. She had been sick for a long time and had visited every doctor and tried all possible remedies, but nothing seemed to have worked. Those who are sick or have family members or friends who are ill, can understand how this woman might have felt. She, like Jairus, had complete faith. Having heard of Jesus' fame and ability she thought, "If I but touch his clothes, I will be made well" (5:28). Her wishes were fulfilled. Jesus, realizing that something miraculous had occurred, wanted the woman to know the cause of her joy. The cure was not magic or some twist of fate or coincidence. No, as Jesus said, "Daughter, your faith has made you well" (5:34a).

In our world, faith on one hand, and fear and doubt on the other, vie for attention and supremacy in our lives, both individually and communally. Each day we are challenged to choose between faith and fear, between confidence and doubt. The Christian person is generally filled with hope and optimism. Over time, however, life begins to chip away on our suit of armor as we experience reality. We get knocked around; the marks of society, its bumps and bruises, begin to appear on us. We begin to lose confidence; hope and optimism begin to wane. We begin to doubt ourselves and others; we even begin to doubt God.

The challenges of life can come in many ways. Possibly we have experienced trials at work — the loss of a contract or the termination of our position. When these things happen we seek answers which many times do not readily come forward. We despair and lose our aggressive ability to do what we can still do. Sometimes the challenges that come are much more severe, like those faced by Jairus and the woman with the hemorrhage. Serious illness or death can strike at any time. We want instant answers and none are available. Again, despair, doubt, and darkness seem to surround us.

Scripture, however, tells us that with faith, the ship that is our spiritual life can be righted, solutions found, and fear conquered. We need to have faith and we also must initiate contact with God to seek that which we need. Jairus and the women with the hemorrhage possessed faith, cast out fear, and came to Jesus with their requests, which because of their faith were granted. Jesus rewarded faith with a healing touch. The same can be true for our ills of body, mind, and spirit.

Once we have experienced God's healing touch then we must pass this on to others. Saint Paul in writing to the church at

Corinth (2 Corinthians 8:14) told the people that they must share God's good gifts with all people: "I do not mean that there should be relief for others and pressure on you, but it is a question of a fair balance between your present abundance and their need, so that their abundance may be for your need, in order that there may be a fair balance" (8:13-14). Today we call this concept distributive justice, the idea that all is gift, even the receipt of healing, and must be shared so that no person is left without adequate measure.

Yes, the darkness of fear and doubt and the light of faith, trust, and joy are in a constant battle for attention and supremacy in our lives. We need to find the faith and trust of those twentieth century pioneers of technology and sport. To say, "It can't be done," to live in fear and doubt, defeats us before we ever begin. We must concentrate on the words of Jesus, "Do not fear, only believe." Jairus and the woman with the hemorrhage found the faith they needed and demonstrated it in their words and actions. Robert F. Kennedy in one of his famous addresses challenged all Americans and the world in a similar way, but in different words. "Some people see things as they are and ask, *why?* I dream things that never were and ask, *why not?*" May we have the courage to believe the same!

Questions To Ponder:

1. Do I see the world as a glass of water half empty or half full? What is my basic philosophy on life, positive or negative?

2. What keeps me from believing that all things truly are possible with God?

3. When problematic situations and challenges come my way, to whom or what do I turn? Where is God in the solution to my dilemmas?

4. When was the last time I assisted a neighbor, co-worker or family member to negotiate a difficult or challenging situation?
5. What examples have I found in my own life or in others that teach me to have greater trust in God?

"Do not, therefore, abandon that confidence of yours; it brings a great reward" (Hebrews 10:35).

Prayer: God, help me to share a positive countenance with all those I encounter in life.

www.ingramcontent.com/pod-product-compliance
Lightning Source LLC
Chambersburg PA
CBHW021334090426
42742CB00008B/604